Safety and Workers' Compensation Strategies

To Unleash Productivity and Profits

Featuring insightful interviews with experts, including Paul O'Neill, the 72nd Secretary of the U.S. Treasury.

Adam Friedlander

ISBN: 1530449812
ISBN-13: 9781530449811
Library of Congress Control Number: 2016904344
CreateSpace Independent Publishing Platform
North Charleston, South Carolina

Contents

Dedication

To caring individuals who safeguard other people's ability to earn a living, capture opportunities, and make a difference.

To Lisa, David and Allie, Bert and Judy, my family, friends, and teammates.

Preface

The inspiring leaders interviewed in this book share a profound caring for the well-being of others and a passionate drive for innovative improvements in processes and solutions.

These outstanding thought leaders discuss innovative safety and workers' compensation strategies that enable businesses to unleash productivity and profits.

The book includes compelling interviews with the following people:

<u>Paul O'Neill</u>, the 72nd Secretary of the U.S. Treasury, serving from 2001 to 2002, and chairman of Alcoa from 1987 to 1999

Bill O'Rourke, president of Alcoa Russia from 2005 to 2008, senior advisor at Value Capture LLC, and coauthor of *The Power of Ethics*

Stephen Newell, partner at ORCHSE Strategies global consulting that services 120 large multinational corporations on safety, health, and environmental matters, and author of the OSHA Blue Book with one million copies sold

David DePaolo, CEO, president, and editor-in-chief of WorkCompCentral.com

Brian J. Connor, partner with the workers' compensation law firm of Weiss, Wexler and Wornow, PC

Peggy Crook, vice president of claims and loss control at Federation of Jewish Philanthropies (FOJP) Service Corporation

Jeffrey R. Fenster, vice president of business development and government affairs at AmTrust Financial Services Inc. and, from 2010 to 2014, the executive director of the New York State Workers' Compensation Board

All the interviews were conducted without advance notice of the questions.

Chapter 1

People's Safety First

Imagine a world where business leaders make safety their top focus. People work without injury. Envision how much more secure people would feel, unleashed from fear, their confidence and self-esteem protected, and their ability to provide for themselves and loved ones safeguarded. People could maximize their productivity and capture the opportunity to make a difference. The organization would thrive.

If only it were that simple. To achieve an injury-free workplace, business leaders must care about safety with unrelenting laser focus.

In reality, many leaders are distracted by the overwhelming daily pressures of running a business. Rather than investing in safer practices and conditions, some treat employees as disposable, placing short-term productivity demands above the needs of people. When a person is injured at work, workers' compensation premiums increase, as do the costs of training and rehiring, and morale and productivity are damaged.

The solution is for leaders to put people's safety first. Not only is this the right thing to do, but it consequently improves productivity and optimizes profits.

In 1991, when my company began forming and selling group-discounted workers' compensation safety groups,[1] we only enrolled organizations with a track record of safety. Their leaders cared about their people and benefited from a true competitive advantage.

In 2006, we broadened our services to help distracted, less safety-oriented employers. "Show me the money," they insisted. Their primary motivation was achieving their financial objectives. Accordingly, we quantified how much their injuries would cost in terms of additional workers' compensation premiums, expenses related to solving morale problems, and hiring and training expenses.

To entice them further, we emphasized that their biggest cost was the lost productivity and profits of not having their "A-team" working. If, for example, an organization performs at only 80 percent of its potential due to employee injuries, the 20 percent in lost productivity dwarfs the other costs.

---

1 Underwritten by the New York State Insurance Fund, 199 Church St., New York, NY 10007.

In 2011, I went to the New Orleans Jazz Festival. The music, food, and celebratory energy were wonderful. While I waited for a friend, I browsed the best sellers at the airport's bookstore. *The Power of Habit,* by Charles Duhigg, caught my attention and ultimately inspired me to write this book.

Mr. Duhigg wrote a fascinating chapter about Paul O'Neill, who, as chairman of Alcoa, created habitual excellence within the organization, starting with safety. "Everyone deserves to leave work as safely as they arrive, right? You shouldn't be scared that feeding your family is going to kill you. Safety should never be a priority. It should be a precondition. Safety should be like breathing."[2] Mr. O'Neill's profound words recalibrated my thinking.

Uniquely in the business world, Mr. O'Neill's focus on safety was not financially motivated. "In a truly great organization, finance is not an objective; it's a consequence of excellence,"[3] he said. In my world, those words are as powerful as astronaut Neil Armstrong's, "That's one small step for man, one giant leap for mankind." Reversing the order of priorities, putting people's safety before financial objectives, was indeed a giant leap.

Of course, that makes sense intuitively, but to successfully persuade business leaders to put people before

2 http://valuecapturellc.com/thought-leadership/ The Irreducible Components of Leadership.wmv.

3 http://valuecapturellc.com/thought-leadership/ The Irreducible Components of Leadership.wmv.

financial objectives, I needed evidence, not just theory. Finally, there was objective proof that it was true.

Duhigg writes in *The Power of Habit,*

O'Neill never promised that his focus on worker safety would increase Alcoa's profits. However, as his new routines moved through the organization, costs came down, quality went up, and productivity skyrocketed.[4]

Alcoa's profits would hit a record high. By the time O'Neill retired in 2000, the company's annual net income was five times larger than before he arrived, and its market capitalization had risen by $27 billion. Someone who invested a million dollars in Alcoa on the day O'Neill was hired would have earned another million dollars in dividends while he headed the company, and the value of their stock would be five times bigger when he left. What's more, all that growth occurred while Alcoa became one of the safest companies in the world. Before O'Neill's arrival, almost every Alcoa plant had at least one accident per week. Once his safety plan was implemented, some facilities would go years without a single employee losing a workday due to an accident. The company's worker injury rate fell to one-twentieth the US average.[5]

---

4 Duhigg, *The Power of Habit,* 108.
5 Duhigg, *The Power of Habit,* 100.

Mr. O'Neill proved that safety is a vital organizational value that generates remarkable growth. The interviews with a broad spectrum of industry leaders that follow are ripe with actionable insights and proven strategies to increase safety.

I've read the interviews many times, and, each time, I gained additional insights into how to optimize organizational performance. I am grateful for the opportunity to share them with you.

Chapter 2

Paul O'Neill Interview

Paul O'Neill is a founder of Value Capture LLC, where he provides counsel and support to health-care executives and policy makers. They share his conviction that the value of health-care operations can be increased by 50 percent or more through the pursuit of perfect safety and clinical outcomes. He was the 72nd Secretary of the U.S. Treasury, serving from 2001 to 2002. He was the chairman and CEO of Alcoa from 1987 to 1999 and retired as chairman at the end of 2000. Mr. O'Neill led Alcoa to become the safest workplace in the world, while increasing its market capitalization by more than 800 percent.

Today, Alcoa operates across more than forty countries at a lost-workday rate that is more than twenty times lower than the average rate for American hospitals. Prior to joining Alcoa, Mr. O'Neill was president of International Paper Company from 1985 to 1987 and was vice president from 1977 to 1985. He served as the deputy director of the US Office of Management and Budget from 1974 to 1977, where he had served on staff beginning in 1967. He worked as a computer-systems analyst with the US Veterans Administration from 1961 to 1966. During his government service, Mr. O'Neill helped shape many of the policies that define the American health-care system today. He serves as a board member at the National Quality Forum, RAND, and at more than a dozen other major corporations and nonprofit organizations.

ADAM: Thank you, Mr. O'Neill. At Alcoa, your intended legacy was safety. To what do you attribute your extraordinary care for people and their safety at work?

PAUL O'NEILL: Well, it starts with an observation of the importance of people and their well-being and actually caring about people and wanting to learn from people, from everybody you encounter.

But then, as I did, when you begin to get a broadened responsibility in an organization (and, for me at least, it was, from the very beginning, a realization)... well, my goodness, these people need me to worry about them and care about them. And as I had more responsibility to assure the safety of their workplace and, in the early days, caring about what was going on at home. People were struggling at home. I didn't want to intrude, but I wanted people to know that I was there for them.

It all flowed from an observation that if people are distracted or unhappy, they're limited in what they can contribute. They're just part of a person, if you will. Maybe they've given the appearance of a full person, but it's a full person with pain, and that's not saying the same as a full person with the stars aligned in the skies.

So it begins on a small scale, and then, the more responsibility you have, the clearer it is that every organization is a function of the alignment of energy of the people who are in it. So the first need is to make sure people are OK and that they are safe, both in a physical sense and in a psychological sense, that they don't feel threatened and in danger by being part of an organization.

It begins to speak to not only one person's relationship with another person, but if you're in a leadership position, to care about whether all people in the organization feel safe and are treated with dignity and respect by everyone who works in the organization. So the more responsibility you have, the more it broadens out into a set of collateral responsibilities to create unity.

ADAM: Can you share your thoughts on leadership and the leader's role in safety?

PAUL O'NEILL: In a broad sense, I think an organization and the culture of an organization are a consequence of the actions of the person in charge. To be clear, it's not only overt actions but subliminal ones and maybe messages that are sent by facial expressions and the like.

Organizations, I think, can't actually be as safe as they could be if the leader doesn't have a personal sense of owning the responsibility of the safety for every person in the organization; it can't create a really safe organization.

ADAM: Can you share your process of how you achieved an injury-free workplace at Alcoa?

PAUL O'NEILL: I started by articulating the idea that we should be an injury-free workplace, because almost every organization that I know anything about, except a few that I know really well, like Alcoa, believe that accidents are inevitable. I don't believe that's right.

I purposefully did something when I was at Alcoa to overcome the idea that accidents are an act of God. I said we won't have "accidents" anymore. If we have something gone wrong, it will be an "incident." And that will give us a license to use our brain to figure out how not to have an incident again. And so I don't accept the idea that injuries to people are providential and that God, after all, wanted you to be hurt on that day. I don't believe that. That's the underlying sense of the word *accidents*—that nobody wanted it, but it was inevitable. So it's really important to flatly say accidents are not inevitable. We may have incidents, but we won't have any more accidents. And we can work on them, and we can cure the reasons why.

And so, it's a beginning place for providing an idea that everyone in an organization can be connected to, because, in truth, nobody really wants to be hurt. Nobody wants to be an accident or an incident. If you can connect with people on the level that's innately human, it establishes kind of a first link in a highway that can connect aspirational goals for everything in an organization: to be the best in the world at everything you do. And personal safety, individual safety, is kind of the first step.

ADAM: After articulating the idea of an injury-free workplace, what would you suggest are the next steps for a small-business owner?

PAUL O'NEILL: I really do think it's an issue that's independent of scale. Even in a two-person firm, it's necessary that people be in good health and not be subjected to injuries. If you're the leader of a two-person organization, you need to have a mind-set that says, "If I'm in charge, it's my responsibility to make sure you're safe." And that means counseling about wearing seat belts. It means assuring that the workplace is truly safe.

In a small manufacturing operation, there's lots of risk. But in a good small manufacturing operation, safety is the first issue every day. Again, it's a way that leaders get connected to people around something that necessarily involves everyone and necessarily involves everyone's brain.

ADAM: How did you communicate the urgency of root-cause analysis and responding within twenty-four hours?

PAUL O'NEIL: Well, first of all, an observation that if fifty people were standing on a street corner and there's an accident, there will frequently be sixty explanations of what happened. It makes an important point that the further away you are in time from an incident, the more unlikely it is that you'll be able to figure out the cause.

The other observation is about what seems to be an organizational artifact that people tend to aggregate things. Knowing that your organization had ten incidents is interesting, but it's not solvable. The ten can only be addressed one by one. It's really important for any kind of thing, including safety incidents, that things gone wrong are investigated as close as possible to real time, one at a time, with an expectation that you can figure out how to adjust the process or the circumstance so that it never happens again.

And it applies broadly, so, as an example, in the wintertime, when the roads are bad—this actually happened on my watch many years ago—we had some sales and marketing people who were in Philadelphia, and there was a snowstorm, and they headed back to Pittsburgh. When they got to the long tunnel that's about forty miles from Philadelphia, the cars were slipping and sliding all over the place, and another car hit them. In lots of organizations, people would say, "That's really too bad," but if you look at it from a perspective of "this should never happen," it suggests people should not put themselves at risk.

In that kind of a situation, the first thing they should do when they get up in the morning is check the weather report and find out what's happening with the weather. If there's a high probability there's going to be freezing rain or snow on the road, they ought to get a hotel, stay until it's better, even if it's a week. Otherwise, they're knowingly putting themselves at risk and accepting the risk as a function of their employment.

In a first-class organization, people will understand their well-being is more important than spending a few bucks on a hotel, and they should always take the safest route, which means don't go at all if there's likely to be danger.

ADAM: Were there unexpected benefits that resulted from your safety efforts?

PAUL O'NEILL: I guess I would say that one of the side benefits of all this was I got to know a lot of people in the organization at remarkably different levels of the organization, because, over time, they all came to believe it was OK to talk to me about these things.

At the beginning, I initiated a lot of it. So if I would see a report on my computer screen in the morning of an incident the day before, and it was not really clear to me, or I wanted to make a point about it, I'd pick up the phone and call the people who were directly involved and talk to them about it.

It was interesting. It made it OK to kind of bust the hierarchy by my initiating the conversation. People began to feel they could initiate the conversation; they didn't have to wait for me.

And that had a great broader consequence for how the organization functioned. It began to help me reduce the hierarchical nature of the organization that things only go up and through a particular channel. That was really helpful. It helped us spread out the ideas much faster.

ADAM: In terms of replacing equipment so people didn't get hurt, was improving productivity part of your plan?

PAUL O'NEILL: I think it had the benefit of improving productivity, but that was not the primary objective; it was a secondary consequence. But, yes, oftentimes when you take out risk, you take out unexpected events.

As an example, let's say there's a factory, and there's an oil leak on the floor, and somebody trips on the oil spot. If the process works right, the root-cause analysis identifies the fact that there was a probable cause to the slip, fall, and trip and maybe a broken bone or something. By fixing that issue, you oftentimes permanently eliminate the possibility of that occurring again. It makes your whole operation more reliable. Your uptime goes up, which is beneficial because you can operate closer to 100 percent capital efficiency, which means you're producing specification-level product twenty-four hours a day, seven days a week. That's the theoretical limit. So in most places, even in some pretty good places, they're more in the 75 percent range.

Every one of these things, whether they're related to a potential safety incident or not, represents an opportunity to get closer to the theoretical limit of capital utilization of 100 percent, so you're always producing perfect product. And so there's an intersection of things that are related to the safety of people and the performance of the organization.

ADAM: Did you find that your concern for your employees was rewarded with their loyalty, commitment, and hard work? Was it palpable, or was it theoretical?

PAUL O'NEILL: I would say it was palpable.

I've been gone fifteen years from Alcoa. But there are a lot of people there who came after I left, who know about what we did, and they're carrying it on, which is a great reward because it makes it then about an institutional force rather than a one-time personality...which is really great.

That's a real legacy, when the culture of an organization goes on in a very positive way when they don't know your name anymore.

ADAM: How do you encourage leaders to strive for zero injuries?

PAUL O'NEILL: Well, I've been privileged to be invited to and have served on lots of different boards. There's almost always an opportunity, as a board member, to talk about what's really important and what needs to be important here.

It's interesting. There are quite a few organizations that I've had something to do with. I'll tell you a little story. I was at a safety conference in San Antonio about three years ago. I gave a speech, and afterward three people in red sweatshirts came up to me and said, "You don't know who we are, but we worked for General Motors. You probably don't know this, but when you were with General Motors, you were loud and clear about safety. As a consequence of the position that you took about the need for a perfectly safe workplace at General Motors, we are really good at safety now, but it was only because you insisted that General Motors needed to adopt a policy of zero injuries to the workforce."

It's interesting how there is carrying power with ideas. I didn't even know about this; I hadn't been on the board at General Motors...I got off in 1995, so this is almost twenty years later, and people are telling me, "You really made a difference because you insisted that they need to become informed about workers' safety."

ADAM: When you discuss safety with various boards, do you discuss safety only as a value, or do you also appeal to their financial objectives?

PAUL O'NEILL: I have consistently said to people over time, "Safety is a leading indicator of all performance at an institution." If you know what the safety performance is, you can be pretty sure that the rest of the performance is not better than the safety performance. At most organizations, that means being mediocre both in safety and at everything else they do, even if they're famous.

ADAM: I agree with you, but what makes you so certain?

PAUL O'NEILL: There are certain qualities of systems that are universal. If you think about safety, individual safety in the context of any kind of organization, it's one of many attributes of an organization. So energy efficiency, environmental efficiency, capital-use efficiency, working-capital throughput, all of those things are different measures of the performance of your organization. I've found safety is the ubiquitous measure that is a leading indicator for everything else.

I would say this in maybe a little bit different way to you: if you find an organization that is truly good at workers' safety, I'd be surprised if you find they're not good at almost everything else they do. On the other hand, if you find an organization that's kind of mediocre or in the middle of the national pack on safety,

I'd be surprised if you find habitual excellence in that organization.

You know, even for companies that make unbelievable amounts of money, they are way underperforming what they could be if they were really excellent at safety.

ADAM: How much did Alcoa grow under your tenure?

PAUL O'NEILL: The market value went up 900 percent in thirteen years.

ADAM: How much of that extraordinary growth do you attribute to your safety efforts?

PAUL O'NEILL: Well, I think it was a combination of the basic tenets of an injury-free workplace applied to everything…working to be at the theoretical limit in everything we do.

ADAM: Which had to invigorate your team?

PAUL O'NEILL: Absolutely.

ADAM: Of what accomplishments are you most proud?

PAUL O'NEILL: It's a shared pride with my wife, being married for sixty years, with four children and twelve grandchildren and nine great-grandchildren. You know, that's the most satisfying.

ADAM: Great. Thank you very much, Mr. O'Neill.

PAUL O'NEILL: Not at all. Good luck to you.

Chapter 3

Bill O'Rourke Interview

Mr. Bill O'Rourke is a senior advisor to Value Capture clients and is a world-leading authority on workplace safety and ethics as keys to high performance. He served in a number of leadership roles at Alcoa. As vice president of environment, health and safety, and sustainability, Mr. O'Rourke helped build the safety-leadership systems that allowed Alcoa to reach world-benchmark status and sustain the continued rate of improvement. As president of Alcoa Russia from 2005 to 2008, he led with safety to achieve dramatic safety and business results in an extremely challenging environment. Under his leadership, the lost-workday rate at Alcoa Russia went from ten times the Alcoa average to better than the Alcoa average, and fatalities, which had averaged five per year prior to Alcoa's acquisition, fell to zero.

Mr. O'Rourke plays an advisory and coaching role to business leaders worldwide. Recent and current roles in addition to Value Capture include being executive director of the Beard Institute in the Palumbo-Donahue School of Business at Duquesne University and fellow of the Wheatley Institution in the Marriot School of Business at Brigham Young University. His book, *The Power of Ethics*, coauthored with Pete Geissler, was published in April, 2015.

ADAM: Thank you for participating, and congratulations on your new and excellent book, *The Power of Ethics*.

BILL O'ROURKE: Thank you.

ADAM: Would you please elaborate on your view that safety is an ethical responsibility of leadership?

BILL O'ROURKE: I believe it's an enlightened leader's responsibility to protect the health and well-being of all employees. That's one of their responsibilities. I think safety should also extend into the community and into product safety and all the other areas where we need to look out for the well-being of customers, suppliers, employees, and all of our constituents.

I think safety is one of the highest forms of treating your employees with the kind of virtue, integrity, and values that enlightened leaders have. A "true" leader needs to sincerely look out for the safety of the employees, give them the tools and processes they need to do their job, and sincerely care about them going home at least in the same condition they came to work. I don't think there is a much higher calling than that.

That, in my mind, is an ethical requirement of most leaders today: to protect the health and safety of their employees. It's not only in the physical safety—and a lot of people think safety is what you do in a manufacturing plant to avoid getting injured. It's also the environment that you create in an office atmosphere that makes sure that these people aren't under undue stress. Stress is OK, but undue stress isn't.

I think the leader's responsibility is to create the kind of climate where employees can thrive, learn, develop, and become better people. And one of the roots of that kind of enlightened leadership is treating your employees, all of them, with dignity and respect, and a form of that is safety. It is the leader's responsibility to give them the safe culture, safe environment, and safety tools so that they aren't injured, whether physically or mentally or otherwise.

ADAM: How has Paul O'Neill influenced you, and did your thoughts on safety begin there?

BILL O'ROURKE: Paul O'Neill has been an ultimate influence on my life, and I'll elaborate on that later.

I was educated as an industrial engineer, so we were exposed to safety. I had my first job after I got out of the US Army at the US Steel Corporation as an industrial

engineer at one of their very large plants, Homestead
Works, just outside Pittsburgh, Pennsylvania. They had
twelve thousand employees there, and that's where I
first got exposed to safety. But I would say it was more
keeping score. It was more of even suppressing incidents, because they didn't want to tell bad news.

I could remember that they bragged about how
many days they had gone without a lost-time injury at
the plant.

I also, as an industrial engineer, was exposed to the
people who were in stretchers in the infirmary. Some of
the company workers went to the injured employees'
homes and carried them into work so that they wouldn't
have to report a lost-workday incident. Meanwhile, these
people were injured. And they were more concerned at
that time at US Steel, I believe—during my tenure, anyway—with the numbers than they were about sincerely
putting the practices of safety into place.

I also got exposed to some of the union-management
committees where it was really a fight, one against the
other. That was not a very good environment for safety
in the plant. My first exposure to safety would have been
in the army, where you are extremely safe on the firing
ranges and places like that; then it was at US Steel.

But for me "safety" really didn't get fine-tuned until I
started to work for Alcoa. When Paul O'Neill came there
in 1987, he spoke about safety every time he talked. The
first words out of his mouth were about safety, whether

it was the board-of-directors' meeting, his executive-council meeting, the annual shareholders meeting, or any meeting. He started it off with safety.

At the beginning, people thought he was phony, and this would go away as soon as the business got tough, but it never went away. And during those thirteen years that he was at Alcoa, from 1987 to 2000, the total recordable rate and the lost-workday rate went down every year that he was there. The lost-workday rate was 1.86 in 1987, which was pretty good for a manufacturing plant—very good, as a matter of fact. He thought that was unacceptable. He brought it down to 0.2 when he left the company.

He did it through his enlightened leadership, in my mind. He really sincerely cared about safety. He also required that the tools, systems, and processes be in place so that people could implement the safe practice throughout the company, everywhere.

I can give you a couple of examples. We had health-and-safety audits in the company at the time when O'Neill came, and they were optional. If a plant manager said, "I want a health-and-safety audit," he would get one. I would say about half of them asked for it. O'Neill said, "This is unacceptable; we are going to make those mandatory." Health-and-safety audits and environmental audits were made mandatory, just as the financial audits and the IT audits were mandatory.

He actually got the audit committee of the board of directors to agree to take responsibility for environmental audits and health-and-safety audits as well. So if a location failed one, the business-unit president had to appear before the audit committee of the board of directors and explain what they were going to do about it. There was sincerity in everything Paul O'Neill did in putting the tools in place.

I can remember working in the safety department when Paul O'Neill was the CEO. We were in the same office building. He would show up early to work, which was usual, and you knew the first thing he did was get onto the real-time safety-data system and check it to see what happened from one day to the next.

If something went wrong, I expected that I was going to get a call. The plant manager was probably going to get a call too, and Paul would want to know what happened, what are we doing about it, and if there is any other information that he should be aware of. So I used to get into work…I tried to get in before him and try to beat that call or try to be in his office or meet him at the coffee station and explain what changes might have happened in the past twenty-four hours.

That kind of reinforcement from the leader really drives safety throughout the organization. It was a great work environment.

ADAM: Can you share your experience at Alcoa Russia, some of the safety challenges and results you had, and why you chose safety to lead cultural change?

BILL O'ROURKE: Sure. This probably goes back to the question of did Paul O'Neill influence you. I remember being asked, can safety leadership be learned, or did you have to be born with it? Well, I learned an awful lot from Paul O'Neill, and I used those learnings when I went on that Russia assignment.

I had been at Alcoa from 1975 to 2005, when I was asked to go to Russia. We were going to conclude the acquisition of two large manufacturing plants. In fact, one was the biggest manufacturing plant in all of Alcoa, and the other one was almost as big. The entire operation had sixteen thousand employees. These were fifty-year-old Soviet operations. The plant in Samara was enormous. It sat on 388 acres, had 129 buildings, the biggest forging press in the world, and the biggest extrusion press in the world. It was really enormous.

Both of these plants we acquired had been neglected since Perestroika, which was about 1993. There was no capital investment, there was no education or training, there was no safety equipment being used in the plant, there were no hard hats, gloves, safety shoes, heat-resistant clothing, anything like that. There were no safety committees. Their incident rate was ten times higher than Alcoa's, and these two manufacturing plants averaged five fatalities a year for fifty years. And that's just on the safety side.

By the way, in these manufacturing operations, everything was wrong. Not only housekeeping, which was an absolute disaster, but you found the pricing was wrong.

They had no relationships with the government or with the communities. The morale in the plants was a disgrace. The compensation systems were not based on any science or any facts or any data. So everywhere I looked, everything was wrong and needed an awful lot of work.

I decided to bring sixty-eight expats from Alcoa from eight different countries from around the world. I knew these people would know the Alcoa values, and they could help instill the values of health and safety, respect for the environment, integrity, financial control systems, etc.

But when I thought back to what O'Neill did when he came to Alcoa, he decided to lead with safety. And safety is what he really led with. He had a theory that if you got safety right, you would get everything right, and that stuck with me.

So I thought, *I have inherited a mess; I'm going to start with safety.*

We formed safety committees in every department and every business that we had there. We required safety meetings by those safety committees at least once a month. We trained eight thousand of the sixteen thousand employees in the first year. We insisted, after the second month, that everybody have and wear their safety equipment. And they did. Their compliance with safety equipment was about 98 percent in the second month.

We focused on the incident rate by bringing in health-and-safety auditors from around the world in addition to sixty-eight expats that we had. We were able to put safe practices in place in every operation throughout the plant. In the housekeeping area, we removed forty thousand tons of steel scrap in the first four months. We made more money on scrap sales than we did on product sales. It was really in bad shape.

We focused on safety and followed O'Neill's example by talking about safety all the time. I tried to do that at every meeting. I would attend a lot of these safety meetings. I would walk around the plant. I would participate in the health-and-safety audits at the two manufacturing locations. By doing that, we were able to have no fatalities in the first full year that Alcoa was there, which was 2006. So they averaged five fatalities a year for fifty years. The first full calendar year Alcoa was there, there were no fatalities—none—which is pretty amazing.

Now the Russians will tell you that was good luck. It wasn't good luck. It was a lot of hard work and effort in putting all the practices and systems and protocols and values in place, and trying to reinforce that system throughout both of the big manufacturing locations. We really drove that.

As I look back today, they're running at an incident rate that's lower than Alcoa's. Alcoa has lost workdays that is now at 0.09, and the lost-workday rate in Russia is lower than that. Their recordable rate is lower than Alcoa's recordable rate, and they haven't had a fatality in seven years.

I think those kinds of results come from building the safety systems and the safety value into the organization in those first three years that I was there, and then having the Russians carry it on as they ran the operations thereafter. So I'm really, really proud that they have been able to carry the safety value forward.

ADAM: Those are amazing results. What was the impact of safety at Alcoa Russia in terms of productivity, morale, and other areas?

BILL O'ROURKE: I think it's dramatic. Some of it is recorded, and some isn't. They have a similar system to workers' compensation in Russia. So when you get the safety record down, of course those rates improve.

By the way, I want to note that Paul O'Neill would never allow anyone to discuss Alcoa's workers' compensation experience. Paul did not want to suggest to anyone that saving money in workers' comp costs was a reason for embracing safety. It was not a reason; it was a consequence. So we never talked about it.

But I think many of the safety benefits are not measured. If you don't have an incident, you don't have a disruption in the operation. For extreme incidents, you can have government officials or others step in and actually shut down your operation. Those kinds of disruptions to your operation are significant. They cost a lot of money. But we don't measure those—the events that don't happen. But you know it's happening whenever you get your rates down to the levels that Alcoa has had. We experienced the same thing in Russia.

A secondary factor is when you stress safety, you are sending a signal, a very tangible signal, that says, "We care about you." What can be better than that? If you tell your employees that you really care about them, then show them in tangible ways that you do, and then they don't get hurt very often in the plant, that drives a culture where, I believe, the morale actually improves over time. Then you build not only that morale, but also you build a pride in the organization: "We are so proud of our safety effort."

In Russia, we distributed our heat-resistant clothing. Everybody wore the jacket, and we put a reflective strip right around the chest area that went clear around the back of this jacket. These jackets are very distinctive, and intentionally, so that you can see the workers in the plant. Well, these workers were so proud of working at Alcoa, they wore those jackets home. I would walk through the streets of Samara, and I would see a couple of people here and there with these blue jackets with the reflective strip on it.

That came from a sense of pride. They were proud to work for this company that really cared about safety. I'm really happy that creating pride in your organization can happen as well.

ADAM: Can you share your safety process, the actual steps implemented, to achieve zero injuries at work?

BILL O'ROURKE: The first step is to have an articulated value or mission statement for your organization.

You need to articulate that to the organization to let them know this is where we want to go. Alcoa, at the time I went to Russia, had seven articulated values. It started with integrity, but one value that was articulated was environmental health and safety, that we work in a manner that respects the health and welfare of the individual and the environment. We translated those seven values into the Russian language and posted them on every building. Just in Samara, you had 129 buildings. When you walked into any building, there in front of you, in Russian, were the seven values of Alcoa. So that's first.

I don't think articulating values or missions or vision statements gets you very far, but I think it's a necessary step. You first let the people know this is what we value, and then you better start putting the programs in place behind it.

So our program started with articulating the safety principles. One principle in safety might be, "We value human life above production." You let people know that's what we value, but then you better show it in your actual practices later on.

We're getting into some of the human-performance systems now throughout Alcoa. One of the rules there is any employee can shut down an operation if they feel that there is danger or high risk. When an employee shuts down an operation, you have to reinforce that that's the right thing to do. Tell them, "You did exactly the right thing." That starts to reinforce the words that you wrote. I think words are important, but actions speak louder.

So you articulate your vision, your values, and your mission, and then you need to articulate principles and beliefs in every area. And I'm talking about safety now, but it also pertains to finance, marketing, procurement, and human resources.

Then you need protocols and standard work procedures that include safety. They need to be communicated and need to be enforced. In addition, you need to have consequences, rewards, and an organization for support. That would mean that there are people who really know safe practices. They know how to get to the root cause of incidents. These resources should be available to others so that they can walk around the operation and assist in driving even safer practices.

Above that, what we had in Alcoa was partnerships with external organizations that could look at what Alcoa was doing. Then you could assess your practices and your results against other organizations. An example of that would be when we created a health partnership with Yale University and Stanford University. The academic curiosity that we got from those institutions was very beneficial. The academics could make observations that a third of your incidents are repeat offenders, which means there are certain people who need remedial training to reduce incidents; 20 percent of your incidents are coming from people who have treatable diseases like hypertension and diabetes.

That raises the question, are you giving these workers the kind of work environment where they can take care of their treatable disease and take their medication, etc.? You can check into that. We looked, and we found out that people who are working overtime in excess of fourteen hours a day or sixty hours a week were getting hurt 25 percent more than other people. So that put in a practice of let's train them at the end of their regular eight-hour shifts so that they have safety reinforced whenever they work overtime. We could require plant managers to realize you are putting your plant employees at risk, so you have to approve this anytime you have people work more than sixty hours a week. That kind of academic curiosity helped us challenge our system all the time and try to make it better and better and better. So those are some of the steps I think you need along the way.

I did mention reward and consequences. Both of those are necessary when you find people who don't follow the safety value of the company. I think in areas involving values, you have to be less tolerant. We all make mistakes, and I think learning by mistakes is good, but you can't make intentional mistakes in an area that's of value to your company, like safety. I would say Alcoa was less tolerant of people who would try to suppress incidents, for example, or not report. You have to step in when those things happen, and let the organization know this is really a value, and you put your job in jeopardy if you intentionally violate some of those premises in the safety area.

ADAM: How did you measure your safety success?

BILL O'ROURKE: In all of Alcoa, we always benchmarked against the best. I remember many trips to DuPont, and they were valuable because you got to feel culture when you walked into any DuPont plant. You get the safety indoctrination as soon as you walk into any building, whether it was an office building or manufacturing plant. You could just feel the safety culture there.

I remember the year that Alcoa's lost-workday rate went below the DuPont rate and how proud Paul O'Neill was that he was able to, at least, tie the best, and then shoot to be even better than that organization. It was a healthy competition between DuPont and Alcoa through the late '90s.

We would look at other organizations, of course, and visit them and try to get better, based on what they were seeing at different places and what practices they were adopting. That's how we came to adopt the human-performance measure. We thought our lost-workday rate was falling so far, and so was the recordable rate. We were almost at an asymptote, and we were trying to find out how we go even further.

The answer that we heard from most organizations, including ORC and others, was you have to adopt human performance. You have to put the responsibility into the hands of individuals, and let them identify what's their high-risk task of the day. Let them raise their hand whenever they think they're in a high-risk situation and need to shut down an operation, and rely more and more on the individual. We have been doing that in Alcoa now. That is our new approach to safety to try and get it even better.

ADAM: What is your exact lost-workday rate?

BILL O'ROURKE: 0.09.

ADAM: What is that a ratio of?

BILL O'ROURKE: It's how many people per one hundred employees, or two hundred thousand man-hours per year, are injured so badly they can't come to work the next day.

ADAM: If they're out multiple days, they're still just counted once?

BILL O'ROURKE: That's one lost workday. Correct. We have added emphasis on another measure; it's called DART. It's how many days you were away when you had a lost-workday injury. And that would help give an indication of the severity of an injury. So if your days away per injury fall to two, that means you're not hurting people very much. Alcoa's is about 1.3 days away per lost-workday injury.

If you went back to the late '80s and early '90s, the DART rate at Alcoa, days-away rate, was closer to six and seven and eight, which meant there were more severe injuries that were occurring at the time. Now there is a good indicator of workers' comp payments as well. It is based a lot on the severity of injury, how many days you're away, as you would know better than I do.

ADAM: How did you avoid compromising safety for profit and production? In other words, it can be a slippery slope as you get more and more distracted by other things. Did you ever find that to be a challenge?

BILL O'ROURKE: Yes, and that's one of the reasons why we had the health-and-safety audit function. The auditors would show up on a regular basis and make sure that there wasn't any suppression of the incidents going on, which is one of the worst situations that can happen. Suppression of incidents would just destroy a safety system, if that was going on. So there was no tolerance for that.

The health-and-safety auditors have ways of correlating people's injuries with the reported injuries in a plant. They could really determine whether record keeping is accurate or inaccurate. That was an important part of the safety culture, to make sure that you had an audit function that would go out and assure that the processes were being followed and the people weren't taking shortcuts, etc.

ADAM: Can a culture of caring about safety succeed without being fully embraced by the leader?

BILL O'ROURKE: I don't think so.

I've seen corporations that have some of the most excellent health-and-safety systems. They have all of the best processes and procedures. They have work-standard practices. They go to root-cause analysis, etc. But whenever you report an incident to the CEO or president or the business-unit president, it falls on deaf ears. When they hold their staff meetings, safety doesn't ever hit the agenda.

Well, pretty soon, the employees start to realize that safety is not really that important. And if it's not that important to the leader, then I don't really have to pay much attention to this. As long as I do the lip service and fill out the forms, it's OK.

Well, our employees are smart people. They know what's going on, and they know what's going on around the world. If something like that happens in Australia, eight thousand miles from New York City, people in North America and Europe, they are going to know what's going on. They talk to each other. There is an informal network throughout the organization that responds to sincerity. If you are not sincere about something, I don't think it's going to go anywhere.

By the same token, if you had a leader who was a champion for safety but had no system, it wouldn't work either. You need to have the process, procedures, and systems in place to support what the leader wants to do. Out of all of that, the most important part is sincere, enlightened leadership from the leader. They really have to embrace these concepts. I really believe that.

ADAM: Some leaders view workplace injuries as an inevitable cost of doing business. Have you found a compelling way to convince those leaders to focus on safety?

BILL O'ROURKE: I've seen examples, and you have to pick your battles at different times. I remember when they were building the new Alcoa corporate headquarters in Pittsburgh. Paul O'Neill took a thirty-one-story high-rise building, and he gave that to the City of Pittsburgh. He built a six-story, large-footprint building between the Seventh and Ninth Street bridges on the north shore of Pittsburgh, very open and modern office.

When the first plans from the construction company came to Paul O'Neill, he reviewed the cost of the building. They had built into the budget $200,000 for one *death* of one of the construction workers during the construction project. And Paul O'Neill said, "What is this?"

They said, "Well, someone is going to die on the job; that's just our experience whenever this happens."

Paul O'Neill said, "No! Get this out of here, and I don't want to see you put it somewhere else. We are not going to injure people on this job. And you're going to see to it that it doesn't happen."

Well, that actually happened. Nobody did get injured on that job. In a three-year enormous construction project, the incident rate was extremely low, and of course, there were no fatalities on that job, which is interesting. So you have to point those out when you get a chance to do it.

Another example is when O'Neill got a report from one of the plant managers, it said, "We are going to reduce our lost-workday rate from this number to this number."

He was pretty upset about that because he told people, "I want your planned number for lost workdays next year to be *zero*, and I want to see it in your plan."

And most people said, "We can't get to zero; we're not going to get there, so I'm not going to put it in my plan; it's unrealistic." They would put in a number.

So O'Neill would go to the plant and call some of the workers together and say, "You know your managers are suggesting to me that six of you are going to get hurt in the next year. Could I have a volunteer from the group that would like to be the hurt employee for next year?"

And, really, what he is trying to do is drive the point home to the leader that it's unacceptable to plan for injuries even though he's a realist, and he understands zero is a lofty goal. You've got to set that as a goal. Anything above it, as a goal, is wrong. He would point that out every chance that he got, which is really admirable. It's hard; it's very hard.

I was asked to speak to a new CEO of a manufacturing operation in the last six months. He wants to have a legacy like Paul O'Neill's. He asked, "What did O'Neill do?" I went through some of the safety practices, the safety concerns, the processes and systems, etc. At the end of our two-hour discussion, he said, "OK, based on everything you said, what percent of my time should I spend on safety?"

My answer was, "One hundred percent."

He said, "I can't spend one hundred percent of my time on safety."

And I asked, "What percentage of your time do you spend on integrity?"

He said, "That's different."

I said, "No, it's not. If you really believe in safety, it's with you all the time. The same way integrity is with you all the time." He didn't like that answer.

You could tell his belief wasn't that this is a value. His belief was that it's a priority that I can give attention to periodically and make it work. Well, that's different than a value. If it's a value, it's with you all the time. It's like breathing. That became contagious in Alcoa.

My observation was that Paul O'Neill taught his leaders to become better leaders. Through his sincere concern for safety, you saw others start to pick up on that and really embrace it. Truly, it wasn't just lip service. These are pretty smart people. They can get by not really believing that. But pretty soon, it became a real culture throughout the organization and still is.

ADAM: What would you suggest to employees who are frustrated by their leader's lack of focus on safety?

BILL O'ROURKE: That's hard. When you get to middle- to higher-level management, even though you are not at the top, I think part of your responsibility is to make your leader a better leader. Point out stories and examples of other corporations and other leaders who have made this work. Challenge them to embrace what they're doing.

At the same time, have an appreciation that their plates are full. They have a full day of work. They are working sixteen-hour days. They're working weekends. They have issues in government affairs and criminal activities, IT security, marketing issues, and costs running wild, and union negotiations are going crazy. So their plate is full. Recognize that. And so is their personal plate. They are probably relocating their family, trying to put the kids through colleges, and so forth.

That's fine, but I think if you challenge them to identify what your values are and encourage them to adopt the values that are good for the company, which includes safety, in my mind. If you can get them to talk about those issues for a while, I think you can make them better leaders.

Then point to examples like Paul O'Neill. Point to books like Charles Duhigg's book, *The Power of Habit,* and the chapter on the legacy of Paul O'Neill and how Paul's habitual excellence in safety has worked and how it has really served people, really well, in certain industries. I think we have to challenge our leaders to be better leaders.

If you aren't successful there, then you take the area that you have. So if you had one manufacturing plant, that's a pretty good area of focus and attention, and you can drive safety in that plant. Maybe teach some of your peers by good example of driving safety in your organization and some of the ancillary benefits of that. Then others might start to adopt it. And maybe even your boss might start to say, "Hey, this is something good that I ought to help drive elsewhere throughout the organization."

If that doesn't work, then sometimes you just have to decide, "I need to work elsewhere." But I think there is a lot of work to do before you make a decision like that.

ADAM: Of what accomplishments are you most proud?

BILL O'ROURKE: The one in Russia, that they continued the legacy of health and safety long after I was gone. I left there in 2008, and here we are, seven years later, and they've gone those seven years without a fatality. That's absolutely incredible! And they have taken their total incident rate down dramatically.

The fellow who succeeded me in Russia, incidentally, ran a can plant in Russia. I got to know him and found out he was a value-based individual. I really enjoyed being around him. He spoke English, and I learned that he was an MD. He actually practiced medicine, but he couldn't make enough money in the Russian system, so he went into manufacturing.

I identified him as a possible successor to me, hired him into the company, and he did succeed me and continued to drive the health-and-safety practices because he really, truly believed in it. I think a lot of that attitude and value came from his medical education. Then he was succeeded by another Russian and has now been made the head of the health department for all of Alcoa, corporately. Isn't that something? He's back into the health business from a corporate basis, which is good for him and the company.

ADAM: What is your intended legacy?

BILL O'ROURKE: I would like to say that I was a values-based leader in the organization.

As you know, I'm speaking on ethics at a number of colleges and universities these days. I have lots and lots of stories from my career that I share with others. I'm learning today that the lessons that I learned were more valuable than I appreciated at the time that they were happening. By being able to share these stories with others, I get more of an appreciation for when times were tough. I mostly stood up to those issues, whenever they were there, regardless of who was in the way, CEO or others.

I've been blessed to have a number of corporate positions such as corporate auditor, head of procurement, chief information officer, and patent counsel. Some of these positions have allowed me to see the corporation from different lights, but they also put me in positions that could get pretty tough. You can imagine in some of those audits of different functions in the organization, you can really get into a hassle with some important people in your company. You have to stand up for what you really believe is right.

I hope my legacy is that I live by the values—all the values, including safety.

As I look back on why I was selected to be the first president of Alcoa Russia, I didn't have heavy manufacturing experience—had a little, but not a lot. The only reason that I would be sent was that I could take the Alcoa values into a difficult environment like Russia. So I think that's why I was selected. I think I was successful on both the integrity side, the financial control side, but mostly on the safety side. That's what I'm really proud of. I think that hopefully will continue to be my legacy at Alcoa.

ADAM: Bill, thank you very much.

Chapter 4

Stephen Newell Interview

Stephen Newell is a partner of ORCHSE Strategies, LLC, a global networking and consulting firm that services 120 large multinational corporations on safety, health, and environmental matters. He heads the organization's highest-level group, the Executive Business Issues Forum, and their Occupational Safety and Health Legal Issues Network; coordinates their main Occupational Safety and Health Group; and contributes to their Global Safety and Health Forum and Corporate Environmental Forum. Steve works extensively with member companies on topics such as fatality and serious-injury prevention, contractor safety and health, improved safety-and-health performance metrics, OSHA record keeping, management-system implementation, sustainability, and safety-and-health value analysis.

Steve joined the organization (formerly known as ORC Worldwide and Mercer HSE Networks) in January 1998. Prior to joining, he was on the executive staff of the federal Occupational Safety and Health Administration (OSHA), responsible for targeting OSHA programmed inspections and measuring agency performance. Before OSHA, he headed the ongoing safety-and-health statistical programs for the Bureau of Labor Statistics (BLS). In both capacities, he had responsibility for the nationwide OSHA injury and illness record-keeping system, authoring the "Recordkeeping Guidelines for Occupational Injuries and Illnesses" many know as the "OSHA Blue Book." More than a million copies were distributed nationwide.

In January 2014, Steve was part of a new leadership team that purchased the health, safety, and environment (HSE) ORC business and now operates under the new banner ORCHSE Strategies LLC. The team remains committed to furthering the safety-and-health mission and to providing the same high-quality level of service, benchmarking, and thought leadership that their members have enjoyed over the past several decades.

Steve obtained his BS degree in economics from the University of Maryland and his JD degree from the Columbus School of Law, Catholic University. He is a past member of the District of Columbia and Maryland State bars.

ADAM: Steve, thank you for participating. How did you become a safety professional?

STEPHEN NEWELL: That's interesting, because I'm a lawyer. I started working for the Bureau of Labor Statistics in a government job. I lived in the DC suburbs. And I went to law school at night, and I started practicing law. I didn't want to go to work for a big law firm; I wanted to go into solo practice. Friends of mine took me in to their law practice. For a while I was doing domestic relations, bankruptcy, criminal law, wills and estates—basically general practice, trying to meet the needs of anyone who walked through our door.

The thing that grabbed my attention was occupational safety and health and workers' compensation. I felt like I could do something *for* people instead of doing something *to* them. At the Bureau of Labor Statistics, I started moving up the chain and getting more involved in the program that was associated with the OSHA record-keeping-and-reporting system.

I ended up writing something called the OSHA Blue Book, which was the agency's official interpretation of the OSHA record-keeping requirements; sort of analogous to the IRS-1040 package that is the government's official interpretation of the federal tax code. They published and distributed about a million copies nationwide.

In my role at BLS, I got to know different people in the safety-and-health community. One was Jerry Scannell, who headed the safety-and-health programs for Johnson and Johnson and later became the head of OSHA. As the Department of Labor's assistant secretary for OSHA, Jerry contacted me and asked if I'd evaluate how the agency used data and information. I did and was hired by Jerry to help improve the ways that they used statistical information. I was on OSHA's executive staff for eight years. Then I went to work for ORC, and it's really been a great gig ever since.

ADAM: What is the mission of ORCHSE Strategies?

STEPHEN NEWELL: That's been an interesting evolution too. ORC was originally a nonprofit organization focused on human resources that was founded in the 1920s by the Rockefellers after they had a mining dispute in which several people were killed. Over time the group evolved to include both a for-profit and a nonprofit entity that held meetings, did consulting, and offered data services.

When the OSHA Act was passed in 1970, they started a new group that would address the health-and-safety needs of their clients. When I was at OSHA, ORC meetings were largely focused on issues associated with regulatory compliance. Infrequently, they would benchmark performance excellence and what companies could do above and beyond the regulations. Now it has really flip-flopped; most of our members consider complying with the regulations as a given and the necessary minimum. These days if you come to one of our meetings and there are ten items on the agenda, maybe one will have to do with regulatory compliance; the other nine are all about effective practices.

In addition to meetings, we have task forces and work groups that address specific issues. For example, we're doing a lot of work to help companies effectively address risk with high-severity potential and prevent fatal and serious incidents. We are also involved in exploring the application of something we call human and organizational performance. It is an exciting space, and we are doing a lot of innovative things that can enhance our profession and contribute to saving lives and preventing human suffering.

ADAM: How do you define safety, how do you measure it, and what benchmarks do you favor?

STEPHEN NEWELL: I'm an old data guy, even though my background is legal. While it's easy to get spooked by the presence of large data sets, I have always looked at data as information in tabular form that, if used correctly, can have a lot of value.

Here's a different twist. When it comes to defining "safety," our profession has traditionally said that safety is the absence of accidents. And that is how we measure it. Most of what our profession does is track either workers' comp claims or OSHA's injury and illness rates, which give us little or no insight into the injury-and-illness-prevention process and how to better manage it. In short, the way we currently define and measure safety is a huge mistake.

The good news is that we are really in the midst of a renaissance in health-and-safety thinking. A good book that provides insight into what we should be doing is *Safety-I and Safety-II*, by Erik Hollnagel. Hollnagel says that instead of defining "safe" as the absence of accidents, safety really should be defined as the presence of capacity. Instead of tracking accidents and/or OSHA injury and illness rates, the way you measure that is by creating and tracking leading indicators. Basically, you want to know if the company or site is doing the right things, if those things are being executed well, and if they are producing the desired results. Many safety-and-health professionals get the concept; the challenge is putting it into practice, determining which are the right leading indicators to use and how best to use them.

The other thing that they struggle with, frankly, is how to properly use the OSHA data. My experience has been that the OSHA data are inconsistently recorded and reported, and that the more pressure you put on them, the worse they get. The accuracy of the OSHA data varies by industry, by company, and even by site. Most employers try to get it right. However, there is enough variation in the data to limit its value for benchmarking and comparative purposes.

Furthermore, increases or decreases in OSHA rates provide very little insight into the quality of an injury-and-illness-prevention process. The OSHA definitions—and I helped write some of this stuff years ago—include cases that are relatively minor and that have limited connection to work. They were primarily designed for general statistical purposes—to get the government aggregate statistics by industry and state to help administer federal and state programs. They were not designed to be used as they frequently are today, as the sole metric to drive and access safety performance.

A few years back, ORC members recognized that the outcome (OSHA) data that they were using had limitations when applied in the United States and were inherently flawed when used globally. One of our metrics task forces developed a new set of outcome measures that was adopted as a new global standard by ASTM in 2014. The focus of the new metric is to track the occurrence of the more severe cases that have a closer connection to the workplace.

ADAM: What is the definition of capacity that you mentioned earlier?

STEPHEN NEWELL: The definition in the high-reliability context of capacity is the organization's ability to avoid serious incidents or, when a serious incident occurs, the organization's ability to rebound effectively.

As I mentioned earlier, OSHA rates provide very little insight into the injury-and-illness-prevention process. Rates may be low due to effective safety programs.

However, they may also be low due to luck or the fact that the company in question doesn't know OSHA's complicated rules for reporting or because the company discourages reporting and/or fosters a culture of intentional underreporting. One of our members once cataloged twenty-five different sources of bias that could impact whether or not a case ever showed up on an OSHA log.

No one knows how accurate or inaccurate the OSHA data are. So if all you're doing is relying on the OSHA data to drive your programs, you're really flying blind, because you have no sense as to whether or not the data are real or what they reflect. That is why you need leading indicators, because, basically, they give a better indication of what the organization is about.

ADAM: What are leading indicators, and which do you prefer?

STEPHEN NEWELL: A trailing indicator tells you what the results are; leading indicators track what was done and how well it was done. If we all agree that injuries and illness are the result of employee exposure to risk, then leading indicators associated with risk identification, risk prioritization, and risk reduction are good candidates. How often do you do risk assessments? If you do a risk assessment, how long does it take you to close out the issues that you've identified?

We are in the process of developing a new approach to doing incident investigations and risk assessments that are more effective in fatal- and serious-injury prevention. That effort includes developing leading indicators around learnings from incident investigations.

Over the years, the method I have used to develop leading indicators is a four-step process. Step number one is to identify the areas that you want to measure. These are the areas that you want to learn about and ultimately influence through driving continuous improvement. Step number two is to develop questions for each one of those areas that you want your measures to answer. Step number three is then to identify candidate metrics that answer the questions that you have listed. Step number four is to pick and choose the best measures among the candidates.

ORC has developed a summary chart for our members to help them think about questions associated with leading indicators at the enterprise level and at the site and business-unit level. At the enterprise level, one might ask, does the company have in place across the enterprise systems and processes that would facilitate site and business-unit-level performance excellence? What this really gets down to is, does the company have a safety-and-health-management system in place, and are the business units and sites getting the right kind of resource support? At the site and business-unit level, the question you're trying to answer is, are the systems and processes being executed in an effective and efficient manner, and are they producing the desired results?

ADAM: Is workplace safety improving?

STEPHEN NEWELL: When they answer that question, most base their answer on trends in OSHA injury and illness rates. And if you follow the OSHA data, the rates for most cases have gone down. Rates for the most serious cases, work-related fatalities, have remained relatively stable.

I believe that safety is improving, but I am uncertain as to the real level of improvement. Why? Because no one, including OSHA, has the faintest idea about the accuracy or inaccuracy of the OSHA data. OSHA hasn't really validated the data in years—in fairness to the agency, in large part because OSHA is generally underresourced, and validating the data is a time-consuming and costly task.

Furthermore, even if the statistics are accurate, we really don't have hard data to explain why the rates have declined. It could be that safety programs have improved over the years. I certainly have witnessed that in our member companies, but they are large global companies with significant safety-and-health (S&H) resources. However, part of the downward trend in rates could also be due to our shift from a goods-producing economy to a more service-oriented economy, or because a significant amount of hazardous work has been outsourced and sent offshore.

All of which lead me to another observation that I find interesting. Although we are perceived as a highly technical profession, much of what we do is not based on hard data. It is driven by experience and intuition.

ADAM: To what do you attribute Paul O'Neill's and Bill O'Rourke's outstanding success at Alcoa, and are safety and business growth correlated?

STEPHEN NEWELL: I think safety and growth are related and that the success at Alcoa largely resulted from a strong safety culture, which was led from the top of the organization.

Of course, I'm a Paul O'Neill believer and view him as a national treasure. He had the vision and the foresight to see that safety could be used as a platform to align and focus the organization and that safety performance was a good leading indicator for overall business performance. Over the years, he made it clear that protecting the health and well-being of his workers was a core value of the organization. As a result, the company was willing to invest the resources and maintain the talent to get the job done.

ADAM: Do you think the leader's passion for safety is critical? And what helps to motivate leaders who may not be focused on safety?

STEPHEN NEWELL: That's a great question. It's got to be more than the passion; it's leadership commitment and support. I've never witnessed a leader who was not good at making the safety-is-important speech. The real question is, do they walk the talk, and are they willing to put resources behind it? And believe me…the people in the organization, from the C Suite to the shop floor, know and can sense the difference.

Unfortunately, in many companies, safety is viewed as a cost of doing business and part of the company's overhead, which leaders strive to minimize as a way of bolstering profits. These are tough economic times when our companies are competing globally, and one of the things they focus on is getting costs down. As long as you look at safety as being a cost or overhead, it's very hard to get true support.

The companies with real leadership support understand, as O'Neill does, that worker protection is an operating philosophy and a way to do business. For him, it's a core value of the enterprise that deserves adequate financial and resource support. That's a big leap for a lot of corporate leaders.

ADAM: Do you think there's a way to encourage leaders to focus on safety?

STEPHEN NEWELL: Yes, I do think there is a way. What we have going for us, first of all, is that morally protecting workers is the right thing to do, and most people want to do the right thing.

Secondly, effective health-and-safety programs bring a great return in business value. Unfortunately, some business leaders are more focused on maximizing short-term profit than taking the moral high ground. So when safety-and-health programs are viewed as a cost instead of a value add, it becomes harder and harder to make the case for new S&H programs and new S&H

investments. In those situations, we need to do a better job of making a business case for what we do. An investment in health and safety is a sustainable investment that will pay for itself.

ADAM: What is the role of regulation?

STEPHEN NEWELL: Even though I represent businesses, I am a strong believer that you need to have strong effective enforcement to deal with those companies that choose to take the low road.

While at OSHA, I worked for Joe Dear, who was the assistant secretary of OSHA in the Clinton administration. After Joe retired, we invited him to speak at an ORC meeting to share his insights and lessons learned from his tenure leading the agency. It was the best civics lesson I ever heard on regulation. Joe's point was that regulations are needed to protect those who can't protect themselves.

Hopefully most of the bigger companies, like our members, are going to do the right thing because they know it's the right thing, they have the resources to do it, and because they realize that investing in worker protection makes good business sense. But for other companies, regulations are really needed to set a minimum floor for protection. Look at OSHA's history, and it is clear that the agency has made a big difference in key issues such as confined spaces, lockout, tag out, falls from elevation, etc.

So on the one hand, regulation and enforcement are clearly needed. On the other hand, it is becoming increasingly clear that OSHA's regulatory model is out of date. I don't think the only way to further safety is by putting more and more regulations in place.

When I was with OSHA, we were involved in an experimental initiative called the Maine 200. The idea was to use data and information to have a meaningful dialogue with employers about controlling risks and abating hazards in their workplace. The approach used data to pinpoint hazards at individual workplaces. OSHA would then contact the employer and try to work collaboratively with the site to ensure the hazards were effectively addressed. If they were, no citations were issued. If the employer refused to cooperate, then OSHA enforcement was applied. The approach was ultimately challenged in court and abandoned by OSHA.

But the principle still has promise, as does the approach taken by the British equivalent to OSHA, the British HSE. In Britain, the HSE has an enforcement arm, but they really try to work with employers before they go the enforcement route. Getting cooperative compliance is a much cheaper way for the government to do business than using enforcement with fines, penalties, contests, and litigation.

ADAM: Why is safety a critical element of business performance?

STEPHEN NEWELL: People realize the human element is critical, and safety is about protecting your human resources. More importantly, it sets the tone for the whole organization.

I've been in this profession for forty years, and to me, safety is a hearts-and-minds profession. Any employer can direct their employees to do a job or a task, and they will comply. However, most of us realize that if people really care about what they're doing, they will do a better job, and they will put more of themselves into it. To me, caring is a reciprocal property. It would be hard for me to care about a business if I felt the business didn't care about me. And so I think health and safety is a key ingredient to business success.

In 2006, ORC was asked by the American Industrial Hygiene Association (AIHA) to build a model that demonstrated the value that industrial hygiene brought to the business. One of our key findings from that study was that the health-and-safety function is a key business enabler. I remember doing a site visit at an Exxon-Mobil refinery in Baton Rouge, Louisiana, and they were doing a major turnaround that impacted a significant portion of their process. If they hadn't had the input from the health-and-safety people as to permissible exposures, they would have had to shut the whole process down, which would have cost millions.

As a profession, we need to understand the true relationship of our function to the overall operation of the business. And we need to remember that we do not "own" worker safety and health. Health and safety belong to the operators, because health and safety is a key to their success. As such, it is best managed as their responsibility and their accountability. Health and safety staffs are advisors, facilitators, and experts; we can help them get the job done. But the operators should "own" it. It's really a core operating philosophy of successful businesses.

That's really what Paul O'Neil was talking about. Safety-and-health performance is a good leading indicator for business performance because health-and-safety systems are very similar to the other systems that are needed to successfully run a business.

ADAM: Can you discuss culture?

STEPHEN NEWELL: Most recognize that a positive safety culture is a must-have element of an effective injury-and-illness-prevention process. The challenge is how to best create one. A short answer is that safety culture is created by the leadership at the top of the organization; safety climate is created by the leadership at the site. Both cannot be generated or sustained by the speeches alone. Culture and climate are created by what the leaders actually do and what they deem important and emphasize in running the business. Culture affects day-to-day decisions, but day-to-day decisions also affect and influence culture.

How does this translate into practical application? As an example, let's look at how companies react to an accident. Those that respond by simply blaming and punishing the injured worker send one signal that influences culture in a negative way. Those that focus on organizational learning send another, more positive signal that the organization is genuinely interested in learning from the incident and preventing ones like it from happening in the future.

The philosophy behind human and organizational performance is that to fully understand an incident, you need to understand the context surrounding it. Since very few workers intentionally try to hurt themselves, to learn from an incident we need to understand, to para-phrase Sydney Dekker and Todd Conklin, why it made sense for the injured or ill employee to do what they did, the way that they did it, when they got hurt. That means that instead of focusing on blaming, shaming, and retraining (or punishing) the injured employee, we should ask, "How did we as an organization let this hap-pen?" which is a very different thing.

Years ago, one of my colleagues, Dee Woodhull, cre-ated a diagram to describe the injury-and-illness-preven-tion process that still works to this day. Basically Dee's point was that the occurrence of injuries and illnesses, or the lack thereof, is not the result of the interaction of the hazard and the controls in isolation. Whether or not an incident occurs is also influenced by the culture, the safety-and-health-management systems, the process conditions, and the human factors, like whether the person has enough training capabilities for doing the job, whether they are fatigued or stressed. All of these things contribute to the organizational context in which the employee confronts the hazard, and each of these elements is influenced by the others. So culture is critically important.

ADAM: In addition to the moral imperative, do you think safety is also about keeping your "A-team" productive?

STEPHEN NEWELL: Absolutely—in more ways than one might originally consider.

My passion for the past several years has been fatal- and serious-injury prevention and changing how our profession and companies address risk that has high-severity potential. In the late 1980s, Dan Petersen, a noted author and safety guru, conducted research that found that fatalities and serious incidents often result from a discreet set of exposures. Dan's research highlighted four: nonroutine events, nonproduction activities, where high energy is present, and in construction turnarounds. And so it's usually upsets and nonroutine situations where someone gets killed or seriously injured.

What I discovered over the years in working with our member companies is that often the worker killed or injured in these activities is one of the best, most senior staff. When the production line goes down and the machine stops, it's frequently the most experienced person who throws himself or herself into the fray to try to get things up and running again. And in doing so, they all too often expose themselves to harm. So I think you're absolutely right, Adam; in many instances there is a direct impact to your "A-team," since they may be the ones who get hurt.

Of course there are indirect impacts too...on everyone involved in the process when someone gets hurt.

ADAM: What is on your safety wish list?

STEPHEN NEWELL: [*laughs*] I'm helping lead a team of dedicated safety-and-health professionals within and outside of ORCHSE to create a new view of worker safety and health. The new view addresses safety-and-health issues in a systematic way and considers an injury or illness as a symptom of problems embedded in the system—the organization. My hope is that we continue to move this effort forward as we convert some of the concepts into tools and approaches that have practical application.

I believe strongly that we need to reexamine what we're doing at almost all levels of our profession. That includes federal OSHA. I worked there for eight years and believe that the agency is populated with very dedicated, intelligent staff who really care about worker protection. But the OSHA model hasn't been revised in over forty years, while the businesses they regulate have changed dramatically. Of course, rethinking the OSHA model is no easy task, given the poisonous atmosphere in Washington these days.

But there is still so much to learn.

As companies and professionals, we may be approaching safety in the wrong way. There seems to be too much emphasis on tracking trends in OSHA rates, and not enough emphasis on learning and on understanding what we should really be doing. The way we traditionally do risk assessments appears flawed, as does the way we do incident investigations, which limits our learning from accidents. The value that we bring to the business is not really embraced. There is much work yet to be done. That said, it doesn't mean that we haven't made progress or that I don't believe in the importance of the safety-and-health mission.

I feel blessed to be in this career and would gladly do what I do every day for nothing. I hope my kids will be as dedicated to their career path as I feel I am to mine.

The thing I never lost sight of, from when I worked at BLS and OSHA to the present day, is that there is a real consequence to what we do. If we do our job right, workers will go home to their families at night as healthy, or perhaps even in better health, than they were when they came into work that day. If we don't, they might be hurt or seriously injured or killed. It's as simple as that.

ADAM: What are you most proud of, Steve?

STEPHEN NEWELL: [*laughs*] My two daughters, of course!

I'm glad that I stuck with this profession. I've been doing this for over forty years. I love what we do, and I love the fact that health-and-safety professionals are generally such caring people. It sounds corny, but I feel so privileged to work with the people I do, not only in my own company, but in our member companies. It may sound like the quote from the movie, *Forrest Gump*, but I feel like getting to know a new ORCHSE member or another dedicated safety-and-health professional is like I'm opening a present. You don't know what's going to be in there, but chances are it's going to be something good.

ADAM: Thank you very much, Steve.

Chapter 5

Brian J. Connor Interview

Brian J. Connor is a partner with the law firm of Weiss, Wexler and Wornow, PC, in New York City. He has practiced workers' compensation defense litigation in New York for twenty-one years, representing the interests of self-insured employers, carriers, and third-party administrators.

He graduated from Boston College in 1991 magna cum laude with a bachelor of arts degree in philosophy. He earned his juris doctor, cum laude, from Boston College Law School in 1994. He is admitted to practice law in New York and Massachusetts and has represented clients before various administrative, state, and federal courts.

Brian began his legal practice with the New York City Law Department, Workers' Compensation Division. While working for the city, he was selected as a "legal rookie of the year" by Mayor Rudolph Giuliani. He sub-sequently worked as in-house counsel for Nationwide and Wausau Insurance Companies and for the Pepsi Bottling Group, focusing on workers' compensation defense. He joined the firm of Weiss, Wexler and Wornow in 1999. In 2011 Mr. Connor was honored as one of the top ten defense attorneys in the nation by AIG/Chartis Insurance.

Brian is a member of the New York Self-Insurers Association and the New York Claim Association. He has lectured extensively throughout the country on workers' compensation matters and frequently conducts file reviews and counseling sessions with employers, carriers, and insurance brokers. He publishes a weekly update on recent case-law developments and industry trends.

He lives in Dutchess County with his wife and two children. He is a supporter of Army and Boston College athletics and is involved in many charitable and community causes, including the Guild for Exceptional Children in Brooklyn, New York.

ADAM: Thank you for sharing with us. Can you please describe what you do?

BRIAN CONNOR: Thank you for having me here. My role is a workers' compensation defense attorney. What I do on a day-to-day basis is represent the interests of employers, insurance carriers, and third-party administrators for workers' compensation claims that are pending before the New York Workers' Compensation Board.

ADAM: What common questions do employers look to you to answer?

BRIAN CONNNOR: I think, depending on who the client is, they have different types of questions. Self-insured employers may ask us very specific questions on particular claims about dollars and cents. What's the best way to resolve a claim? Should this case be settled versus litigated? What is the best way to reduce our ultimate exposure?

With other employers who have an insurance carrier, the questions tend to be a little bit different. Sometimes they want to know if their insurance carrier is doing a good job in administering their claims or not, to get an unbiased outsider's opinion. They may want us to get involved with that carrier to formulate strategies for best resolving and handling cases.

Other employers may have questions on more of the labor-and-employment side, personnel type of issues. For example, taking people back to work with a light-duty type of position or a transitional position—how is that done, and what's the best way to accomplish that? We get questions about job terminations a lot—are they allowed to terminate somebody who is out on workers' compensation? What are the ramifications of that?

ADAM: What's your feedback on the termination question?

BRIAN CONNOR: New York is an employment-at-will state. If an employer wants to terminate an employee, generally they have the right to do so. What they need to be cautious of, in terms of the workers' compensation law specifically, is to make sure that any termination is not done in a discriminatory manner as the result of that employee pursuing a workers' compensation claim. Section 120 of the Workers' Compensation Law prohibits any type of employer discrimination against injured workers as the result of them bringing a workers' compensation action.

Ultimately, the law anticipates that employers need to replace workers. If somebody goes out of work on a workers' compensation injury and the employer needs to bring somebody in to replace them, that may be an instance where separation from employment is the only way they can go about that, to hire somebody who would fill that slot. An employer can't be expected to keep a slot open permanently for this person to potentially return to work.

Looking beyond the issue of separation from employment, a lot of times employers may want to keep the person on the books, because a big part of cost savings is return to work. In an ideal situation, you want your employees to come back to work and to be productive. Whether that's ultimately in a full-duty capacity or on a transitional basis, it's really an important way that employers can reduce their exposure on any claim.

I think employers need to understand just how important that is to their bottom line. If you can get people back to work, keep them productive, and get morale in the workplace up, you are not only going to have cost savings on that particular claim, but you are probably going to get more productivity and have better work morale overall. That might prevent future claims from happening or prevent people from potentially exaggerating their existing claims.

ADAM: If the employer needs to terminate the injured employee, are they vulnerable legally?

BRIAN CONNOR: An employer has to take into account several things; only one small aspect is workers' compensation. There are also labor and employment issues that may come into play. There may be union-contract considerations. Everything needs to be considered before any type of separation from employment is acted upon.

In terms of people bringing discrimination complaints within the workers' compensation forum, injured workers have a very high burden of proof to prove they were discriminated against. I would say for the vast majority claims that are brought under Section 120, they are not established against the employer. Yet you can't prevent employees from bringing claims of discrimination in the first place, and the defense of these claims can prove costly in terms of both time and money.

ADAM: Many employers viscerally dislike workers' compensation costs. Do you think they underestimate the benefit of the legal protection it provides as the exclusive remedy?

BRIAN CONNOR: I think a lot of employers don't appreciate the exclusive remedy that workers' compensation provides. Exclusive remedy basically means that if someone is injured in the course and scope of employment, that the employer generally is immune from a direct lawsuit by that injured worker. The exclusive remedy simply indicates that the worker can only get benefits from workers' compensation.

If there is a third party who might be responsible for that injury, who is not the employer, the injured worker can still bring a lawsuit against that third party. Only in very limited circumstances can that employer be pulled into that legal action. Generally speaking, that is either through the existence of a "grave injury" or if there is some kind of contractual relationship between the employer and the third party.

Employers start to realize the value of exclusive remedy when they discuss with their carrier or their defense counsel whether or not a particular claim should be denied. An employer may ask the question, "Can we deny this injury that occurred for this particular worker?" Possibly they have a legal basis for denying the claim, but then if workers' compensation doesn't apply, they now have to look at the potential exposure they face from a direct lawsuit under a negligence theory by that injured worker.

We see this with employees who slip and fall on the premises that might be owned by the employer, and the employer wants to deny it because the employee was on an unpaid break. What they have to understand is that if that employee does not have the ability to collect workers' compensation, based on the denial of the claim, that person can now proceed as a member of the general public. If there was a hazardous condition that they can prove existed, well, now you are talking potentially big dollars in a liability suit.

So ultimately, workers' compensation can protect employers from lawsuits by their employees. At the same time, it has a much lower burden of proof for injured workers to collect benefits if it is a compensable injury. That goes back to when the workers' compensation law was first enacted. It was the great compromise: employees lost their right to bring direct lawsuits but had a much easier burden of proof to collect benefits, and employers were shielded from those direct lawsuits but will now have to pay workers' comp benefits, essentially based on no fault of their own, because people got injured at work.

ADAM: Since the system is designed to compensate workers, does that mean employers are "behind the eight ball"?

BRIAN CONNOR: I don't think it necessarily means they are "behind the eight ball," but there are a lot of presumptions that are in favor of the injured worker.

Employers are really pressed to investigate their claims very quickly. I won't say that they are prejudiced as a result of this expedited process, but, certainly, there are cases that would benefit from a longer stretch of time to develop the record in much more detail than the Workers' Compensation Board might allow.

It's not really a level playing field that we are dealing with, but that's the way the statute was created. I think employers need to look at a lot of cases as not necessarily a win-lose proposition, but in terms of how they can reduce their ultimate exposure. That doesn't necessarily mean having every claim disallowed or having benefits suspended on every case that comes up for litigation. It's really looking at the bigger picture and trying to determine how to get the cases closed in a cost-effective and efficient manner.

ADAM: Can you discuss any cases that are educational or memorable?

BRIAN CONNOR: I know people always love to cite the fraud cases that they found over the years as examples of victories. Certainly, I can give you examples of fraudulent cases of people who were caught on videotape injuring themselves intentionally, other people who have returned to work off the books at different places who have been caught by the employer, and people who have lied about their medical conditions or their preexisting conditions in order to enhance their claims. Those are the cases that make headlines to the employers.

I think a lot of victories are achieved not necessarily on the big, splashy cases, but on ones that can be resolved before they ever get to the point of being these ugly, nasty cases that require a lot of litigation.

Some of the most memorable cases we've had have been ones where the employer has created light-duty jobs for the injured workers to return to. Employers have to be creative about this. Maybe the person has some kind of very severe medical restrictions on what they can and cannot do, but some employers have really gone out of their way to create positions that accommodate those restrictions and disabilities. We have seen great instances where people have returned to work on a transitional basis during the healing process, and two, three, or four months before they are fully recovered and able to come back to work. The success there is the fact that they were able to come back to their original employment, without restriction, and became productive members of the company once again. Otherwise, the employer works to find a permanent job that accommodates their restrictions with a different job title, somewhere else in the company.

There was one case where a permanently disabled claimant did not want to settle a claim because his wife was out of work, and the fear was that the family income would dry up if he settled the workers' compensation claim. Rather than abandoning the idea of settlement, however, the employer paid for a job-placement service for the claimant's wife. When she secured a new job as the result of this placement service, the claimant was willing to proceed with a settlement that was favorable to the employer. It ended up being a good investment to reduce the employer's ultimate exposure.

ADAM: The theory about early return to work is that employees will want to return to their full-time position sooner than if they just stayed home. From your experience, is that the case?

BRIAN CONNOR: Absolutely. Getting people back to work and productive within the company helps everybody involved. If you can accommodate someone's restrictions, at least on a transitional basis, it gets them out of the house and back to the workplace. They have less time to brood over the case while they are sitting around not doing anything. It makes them feel that they are valuable.

The best situation is when an employer wants an injured employee to come back to work, and they work with that injured worker to find a spot that fits their restrictions, instead of having some employers who literally turn their back on the injured workers, never speak to them, and never want to hear from them again. Those are the types of cases that can really turn bad over the course of time, with consequential injuries and psychiatric overlays. Employers derive a benefit from having somebody being somewhat productive. Even though they have to pay them salary, the claimant is not getting paid workers' compensation indemnity benefits. The fact is the employers are getting something for their money when they bring the person back on a light-duty or accommodated position, as opposed to just paying out the indemnity benefits for a person sitting at home.

I think, as you mentioned, Adam, that reconnection that can exist between the worker and the employer is important because they feel like a valued member of that community. They get to keep up the relationships with their coworkers and their managers or subordinates. In our experience, getting people back into those roles really helps with the overall healing process, in terms of getting them back to be productive members of the workforce, which is ultimately the goal of workers' compensation—to get people healed and working again.

ADAM: What are the best practices for employers?

BRIAN CONNOR: Best practices can start even before they hire somebody—doing a background check and possibly drug screening and physical-fitness testing for certain types of jobs. This will help to weed out people who might be poor candidates, untrustworthy, or prone to injure themselves.

Once people are on board, I think the best practice is to make investments in safety and training, because obviously, the least expensive claim is the one that never happens. It's really hard to prove whether or not an investment in safety training and procedures is cost-effective, because you don't know how many claims you are avoiding by making that investment. But certainly, if an employee feels like the employer is doing everything they can to protect them, they feel like a valued member of that community, of that family, and they are probably less likely to report a claim as workers' compensation that might otherwise be unrelated to work.

One example of that is an occupational-disease type of injury. Let's say someone wakes up one morning at home, and their back hurts. They are fifty years old, and their back has been hurting on and off for the last few months. They can do one of two things: they can simply chalk that up to the aging process, to general wear and tear of life, and treat the back condition through their regular insurance plan; or they can decide to claim the back condition is the result of a workers' compensation occupational disease, based on whatever it is they do on a daily basis. Occupational-disease claims are sometimes hard to defend, given the presumptions of the workers' compensation law and the favorable treatment given by the board to a lot of injured workers. Once again, if the employee really feels like they are valued at work, they are probably less likely to blame the employer for these unrelated medical conditions. They are more likely to just accept the responsibility themselves and go on with life.

Other best practices occur once an injury occurs. The worst idea would be to just simply ignore the injured worker, don't make contact with them, separate them from their employment, and just cast them adrift. Those are the cases, more likely than not, that will turn into really high-exposure permanent-disability claims.

The best practice, once the injury occurs, is for the employer to keep reaching out to the injured worker at home, to let them know that they are valued, to let them know that the employer is actively awaiting their return to work, and they are willing to make accommodations to bring them back on a transitional basis. Also, by keeping up that line of communication, it helps employers to learn the motivation of the injured worker: are they motivated to stay home and make this a bigger claim than it really is, or are they motivated to get better and come back to work? Without that line of communication, really, the employer has no idea.

In terms of best practices when a claim is reaching the conclusion, if you are doing a Section 32 full and final settlement, make sure that before you enter any final agreement, the person has been separated from employment on a formal basis. Because once you enter that Section 32 agreement, you may be paying this person $100,000 or more; you don't want them to come back to work two weeks later and be reinjured and then start this process all over again.

ADAM: Do you think that employers' culture plays a role in the claim's occurrence and outcome?

BRIAN CONNOR: Absolutely. If an employer tends to treat their people as being disposable, those employees, if they are injured on the job, are far less likely to want to return to work for that employer, because maybe they never liked their job in the first place; they never felt appreciated and valued as an employee. Instead it gives them motivation to stay home and try to reap as many workers' compensation benefits as they can.

A lot of employees may blame the employer for the injury. Once you get that blame mentality, moving forward becomes a very adversarial process, and it is unlikely, at that point, that people are going to come to a meeting of minds, with an accommodation or with some type of return to work that would be useful.

If the employer has a culture of safety, invests in safety training and equipment, and asks employees for input on how to make the workplace safer, employees are going to be less likely to be injured and assign blame.

ADAM: Do you think some employers consider employees as "disposable" because they perceive the cost of safety is greater, that their company will be more productive simply replacing injured employees than by building a culture of caring that keeps their "A-team" working and safe?

BRIAN CONNOR: In my opinion, employers that feel their employees are disposable and that it is cost-effective need to reevaluate how they are running their company. Their perception that they are saving money may be very flawed, because they may have a much higher incidence of injuries and much higher exposure for those injuries that do occur. If you ask any employer what they value most from their employees, I think most employers would value loyalty among the highest of qualities. By treating people as disposable, there is no loyalty there.

In terms of running a successful business practice, most of the major corporations treat their employees well. They reap a benefit from that, which may not be tangible in terms of dollars and cents that you can necessarily prove, but it's a question of doing the right thing, as opposed to acting solely for what they perceive to be the financial benefit of the company.

ADAM: What can employers do to make your job easier?

BRIAN CONNOR: From employers directly, the first thing that we would ask them to do is be honest and forthright. We get a lot of employers telling us things that they think we want to hear, which turns out to be completely incorrect. When we move forward with the litigation process, it backfires against them. As defense counsel, we don't like surprises, and the more forthcoming an employer is, the better we can do our job, and that also translates to the insurance carriers that are handling the case. Don't withhold information because you think it might be damaging to your position. Just lay out the cards as they are, and then we can better figure out the right strategy to deal with it.

ADAM: You mentioned mistakes you think employers are making with their handling of claims, but is there anything you would like to add?

BRIAN CONNOR: In terms of the actual handling of the case, I think it's best to let the insurance carrier and the defense counsel formulate the best strategies. Sometimes employers become extremely aggressive, and they want to control the litigation process on a claim. Without the full knowledge of the workers' compensation law, that employer is going to misdirect the litigation by becoming too involved or may start to form an adversarial relationship with the carrier or defense counsel, and that is just a very unhealthy place to be.

ADAM: Do you see a lot of fraud?

BRIAN CONNOR: On a percentage basis, we don't see a lot of fraud. In order to prove fraud in New York, you have to show that someone made a material misrepresentation of fact for the purpose of influencing workers' compensation benefits. Unless you really catch someone in a complete deception, it's difficult to prove.

The fraud cases that we see prosecuted successfully generally involve ones where you have absolute, clear proof that someone is lying on the record. Those are the cases where you may have a claimant out of work and disabled, and video surveillance is taken to show that person has, in fact, returned to work doing something else and has not reported that work activity to any of the parties. Those are clear instances of fraud, and those need to be vigorously prosecuted in order to send a message to other workers who might think of doing similar things in the future.

When it comes to the medical issues, the board is much more likely to characterize findings of medical doctors, versus the actual day-to-day activities of a claimant, as just being nonfraudulent in nature. It is just having a good day or just slightly embellishing the claim, which might not necessarily rise to the level of fraud.

It's hard to define which cases are going to be clear fraud cases, but you know it when you see it. I think that's the way defense counsel, most carriers, and certainly the board looks at it. If you look at a case and it's just crystal clear that someone is lying, then those are the cases that will be taken up on the fraud issue.

ADAM: How do you distinguish fraud from abuse?

BRIAN CONNOR: There is a fine line—all fraud is abuse, but not all abuse is fraud. Fraud is an extreme abuse of the system, one that carries with it an intent to deceive. If you can show someone is abusing the system, even though it may not rise to the level of fraud, you can still introduce evidence in support of your position to gain leverage on a case.

Let's say you obtain surveillance that shows that the injured worker is more physically capable then he or she told an independent medical examiner. On a case like that, maybe you introduce surveillance, not so much to prove fraud, but to prove that the level of disability is actually far less than what the treating doctor is saying. You are doing it to bolster the carrier's position to either ratchet benefits down or to cut benefits off altogether.

ADAM: What have you found to be effective in fighting fraud?

BRIAN CONNOR: A prudent use of surveillance is the best tool in fighting fraud, presuming that the fraud has to do with somebody misrepresenting themselves as either not being active in the labor market or exhibiting an extreme level of disability. Video evidence speaks for itself, and if the claimant doesn't really have a rock-solid explanation for what this video shows, those are the cases that are much more likely to be successful.

That said, I think surveillance needs to be used selectively. It's expensive, and most surveillance efforts don't result in any positive findings. Employers and carriers need to target their surveillance efforts on cases where they have a real suspicion that something fishy is going on. There are lots of red flags. For example, if we get an independent medical exam that says this person has absolutely no disability and that they appear to be malingering or exaggerating their symptoms to an extreme degree, that may be a red flag for a carrier to say that they should go out and get surveillance. People leave anonymous phone calls with carriers or employers saying, "Hey, I caught John Smith working at this place yesterday; you may want to look into that." Obviously that is something that should be followed up.

Social media is a very inexpensive way for people to see whether individuals are engaged in any type of activities that might rise to the level of fraud. For example, if you go on somebody's Facebook, Twitter, or Instagram pages and see that they are planning on going skiing, yet at the same time, they are claiming they can't return to work at their sedentary employment, that now actually gives you a targeted reason to conduct surveillance on that day. It's actually amazing the amount of stuff people put on social media without any type of protection or privacy whatsoever. It's a good way to keep tabs on people.

ADAM: Why do you think employers believe most claims are fraudulent?

BRIAN CONNOR: We read in the news a lot about workers' compensation fraud or social-security fraud or all types of different fraud. You tend to think that your own people must be conducting the same type of fraudulent activity.

But I think it is a tiny fraction of cases. Most people who sustain legitimate injuries at work are not trying to take advantage of the workers' compensation system. Most people are attempting to get themselves back to work and recover as quickly as possible. It's those few cases that grab all the attention that make people think that fraud is pervasive.

ADAM: Do you think employers and employees have unrealistic expectations of the system?

BRIAN CONNOR: That is a good question. In our experience, people do go into the process with unrealistic expectations as to what can be accomplished. That's on both the injured worker's side and the employer's. They expect decisions to be made by the board quickly. They expect that whatever medical witness that they present will be deemed credible. They anticipate that the board is like a court that you see on television, *Law and Order* or some other type of legal show, where, in fact, it is just not the case. The board has very little time when hearings are scheduled to devote to each individual claim. There is a lot of volume moving through the system. The amount of attention the board might give to a particular claim may strike people as being abnormally or critically low.

Everyone believes they are going to prevail when a case enters litigation. But in reality, once a case enters the litigation process, one party is going to win, and one party is going to lose. A decision of the board, however, only needs to be supported by a preponderance of the evidence or substantial evidence. Even though you may have a strong position, the other party also may have enough evidence to support its position. If your expectations are unrealistic, it can be a frustrating process.

ADAM: What is on your workers' comp wish list?

BRIAN CONNOR: As defense counsel, my wish list is the same as the carriers and employers. In New York, a lot of employers and carriers are pushing for the board to reassess how schedule losses of use are determined pursuant to the medical-impairment guidelines. A schedule of loss of use is essentially an injury to an extremity that results in a permanent loss of function. That will translate into a number of weeks of benefits at the conclusion of a claim when a person reaches maximum medical improvement.

For decades, the board has relied upon a set of medical guidelines to assess these schedule losses of use, in terms of how severe they are and how many weeks of benefits would be awarded to an injured worker. But these schedule-loss-of-use guidelines are based on, let's call it old medicine, where somebody who has a knee or hip replacement is automatically entitled to get, we'll say, a 50 percent schedule loss of use of that extremity. Medical science has advanced to such a degree that people can now get knee or hip replacements and be restored to almost exactly the same function that they had before the injury. One wish is that the board reevaluates those guidelines and brings fresh medicine into the perspective.

In terms of how the board functions on a day-to-day basis, the wish list is the same for everybody: that the board can somehow make their system work better in terms of efficiency. People, when they request hearings at the board, whether it is an injured worker or carrier, sometimes have to wait months before the board reacts. During that time, if you are the employer, you may be paying ongoing benefits, or, if you are the injured worker, perhaps you're not being paid benefits and not getting the medical care that your doctors have been requesting. That's a problem.

Also, having the board expedite the appeals process is a huge step that needs to be taken. Right now, when a carrier or claimant files an appeal, it may take up to a year, sometimes even more, for the board to make a final decision. In the meantime, the case is essentially in limbo. That type of efficiency would be useful to everybody.

One thing on my wish list that would go against the board's newest initiatives would be to move away from video hearings. In the last year, the board has made a strong push to try and make many hearings be with the judge appearing remotely. The parties that go to the Workers' Compensation Board look at a television screen and have the judge make rulings, even though the judges are not physically present there. I think the more you detach the judges from the hearing process, the less effective the process becomes. You need a judge to have some kind of personal, live interaction with the parties, rather than by video, in order to assess issues of credibility and in terms of getting a real perspective for the case.

The process is now trying to expand this to allow injured workers and attorneys to appear by video. At one point, there will literally just be a virtual hearing; nobody will need to be at the Workers' Compensation Board. While I give the board credit for the technological advancements, I think it is losing its personal touch and humanity. If I were an injured worker, I would want a judge there, live and in person, to listen to me and to hear what I'm saying, as opposed to just being on a video screen.

Those are on my very short, abbreviated wish list. I can go on all day talking about things that could be changed or modified to make the system better.

ADAM: Is there anything you would like to add?

BRIAN CONNOR: I know you have always been an advocate of creating a caring work environment as being one of the elements of success, and I couldn't agree more.

As defense counsel, one of our jobs is always to look for ways to bring about a cost-effective and expeditious resolution to claims. Employers should be encouraging the carrier, to whatever extent they can, to intervene early to bring about final resolution of matters. The longer a case stays open, generally, the higher the potential exposure. The best claim is a closed one.

The key to successful litigation is knowing how to get leverage on a case and then knowing how and when to use that leverage to your advantage. That is the benefit to working closely with defense counsel and claim administrators—identifying your leverage and finding a way to use it intelligently. In our current environment, it is more important than ever for the employer, its administrators, and its defense counsel to work together as a team to bring about the best results.

The more employers can educate themselves on this whole process, the better understanding they will have, and when it comes down to working as a team with their carrier and defense counsel, everyone will ultimately be aligned as to where a particular case needs to go. Once the parties can come to an agreement on strategy, the more successful they are going to be.

ADAM: Brian, thank you so much.

Chapter 6

David J. DePaolo Interview

David J. DePaolo founded WorkCompCentral in 1999.

Mr. DePaolo became a member of the California State Bar in 1984 and practiced workers' compensation law in California in private practice prior to starting WorkCompCentral with Miller & Folse, Adelson Testan Brundo & Popalardo, and as a sole practitioner.

Mr. DePaolo holds a JD from Pepperdine University School of Law (1984), a master's in business administration from California Lutheran University (1997), and a bachelor of arts in English from San Diego State University (1981).

His civic and professional organization involvement includes the Los Angeles, Ventura County, and Conejo Valley Bar Associations; Ventura, Conejo Valley, Oxnard, and Port Hueneme Chambers of Commerce; Boys and Girls Club of Port Hueneme (he has held director and executive offices); USCF; NORBA; and Hueneme Surf Sailors Association. He has been honored for his community service by the Ventura County Board of Supervisors.

Mr. DePaolo has been widely published on the topic of workers' compensation, including the *Journal of the International Association of Industrial Accidents Boards and Commissions, CWCE* magazine, the *Claims Examiner* magazine, WorkCompCentral, and WorkCompSchool.

Mr. DePaolo has lectured and/or provided expert guidance on workers' compensation issues to the Council on Education for Management, the Texas Insurance Council, the *Los Angeles Times*, Dow Jones News Service, Fox News, Employers' Fraud Task Force, *Fortune* magazine, the California Association of Rehabilitation and Reemployment Professionals, and more.

ADAM: David, thank you for participating. What prompted you to leave your workers' compensation law practice and start WorkCompCentral?

DAVID DEPAOLO: WorkCompCentral was originally started to promote my law practice. I had the website up for a couple of years, and I practiced workers' compensation defense law for about eighteen years. It provided a source of living, but it certainly wasn't my ideal career.

Out of the blue, in August of 1999, one of my now–business partners called me up; he had noticed the website and thought there was something with it. He asked if he put together some financing, whether I would be willing to quit the practice of law and do this full-time. That was it; that's how I got started.

ADAM: Do you have any thoughts on safety or workers' compensation strategies that could improve the productivity of employees and the bottom line for employers?

DAVID DEPAOLO: Well, I do. It just comes down to one single thing: that's your employee. So if you take care to ensure, obviously, the safety of your employee in the performance of the job, but if an accident does happen, you also go that extra mile and demonstrate to the employee, with employment practices, that you care about that employee, you're going to end up with a more productive employee, a quicker return to work, a faster recovery from the injury, and a lower experience modification on your workers' compensation premium.

It doesn't take a whole lot of effort to demonstrate that there is a caring attitude. A card from the CEO while recovering, assigning a liaison or somebody specific to go knock on the door of the injured employee every couple of weeks to bring some flowers or a cake and just see how things are going, a telephone call every once in a while to check in.

And then also to manage the claims process to make sure that the claims administrator, whether it's a third-party administrator or an insurance company's claims house, is not jockeying around with the employee and making sure that the appropriate medical treatment is authorized, without delay, and is followed up with some quality assurance.

ADAM: On your blog, you mention "a new paradigm in worker injury protection." Could you please elaborate on that?

DAVID DEPAOLO: Well, I think what's going to happen over the course of the next ten or twenty years is an integration of the medical component of workers' compensation with general health insurance. In other words, right now we have, in the United States, many different silos of medical care. You have, obviously, your general health care and workers' compensation; those are the obvious ones.

But if you get in an automobile accident, there is a medical-care component to that. If there's a slip and fall on somebody else's property, there is medical care involved in that. All these different factions, all these different silos of medical care, they fight with each other, which causes unnecessary delays in treatment and, as a consequence, frictional costs that ultimately result in a greater expense for either the injured worker, the employer, or whoever is paying for the services.

It's just not a tenable working model for the future. It just cannot continue to exist, simply because people aren't going to put up with it anymore. So I see integration in health care with the delivery of services being first and foremost to whoever gets injured, whether it's an employee, an employee's dependent, and so forth. Then, the "white collars" will figure it out on the back end, and they can fight about who is getting paid or who is responsible for getting paid.

Then all that leaves you with, in the end, is some disability component. I think that's going to change too. I think the attitude is coming around that it's not disability that we should be rewarding; we should be rewarding ability. We should be rewarding productivity. We spent one hundred years figuring out how to reward disability, so we're not going to figure out, instantly, how to flip that coin and reward productivity, but somebody will come up with a formula and will test it.

I'm sure that we'll come up with a better way of dealing with this whole thing. Because we are not dealing anymore with what was the original premise of workers' compensation, which was an accident that caused some trauma. The whole nature of work, the employment relationship, how people interact with each other, and what we actually do now for work have all completely changed. So we need to take a look at these social systems, whether they are privatized or government backed, and rethink the model, and come up with something that is going to better serve society.

ADAM: Since all workers' compensation costs start with workplace injuries, why do you think there isn't more focus on improving safety from the employer's perspective and the carrier's perspective?

DAVID DEPAOLO: I think there is a huge focus on it, but what is probably the missing component is education—just how far things can be taken relative to the safety component. What sort of incentives can we put in place that aren't going to violate law or cause some sort of discrimination lawsuit to happen that can promote safe practices and reward employees for engaging in safety? So you have all these different governmental agencies. You have OSHA; in California, you have Cal/OSHA, which is an even more refined OSHA thing. You have safety watchdogs. I think the incentive is there for safe practices.

Again, it's an employer education thing. For instance, the oil industry in North Dakota; they have a terrible track record for safety. That's because nobody knows who the employee is anymore. The accountability for employee safety is passed through many different layers of subcontracting groups. The accountability for safety gets diluted. I'm just using that as an example, but safe practices with the North Dakota fracking industry is going to take some effort and probably governmental regulation and discipline on those companies to shore up the accountability and responsibility for safety.

ADAM: Does it cost more to fight fraud than is saved, and, if so, should it be fought anyway?

DAVID DEPAOLO: Well, what kind of fraud are we talking about? There are so many different types of fraud. Most fraud prosecutions go after the low-hanging fruit, which are injured workers who are working while they're supposed to be temporarily totally disabled. That is easy to find; it is easy to prosecute but, frankly, does not have a good return on investment.

Then you go up the food chain to provider fraud, where, as an example, Michael Drobot and Pacific Hospital of Long Beach were implanting forged spinal hardware into patients that probably didn't need that surgery and paying kickbacks to the physicians for each surgery that was done. And that results in hundreds of millions of dollars of fraud.

And then, you can go further up the food chain to, for instance, when the brokerage community got caught with bid rigging and forging policy bids for coverage to ensure that the company that paid the higher commission was the one that was selected. So you have all sorts of different fraud. They require different levels of investment and require different levels of commitment.

I think there needs to be careful consideration as to the fraud-allocation dollar. You don't want employees running amok and claiming injuries that never happened and pursuing disability that isn't there. But at the same time, from a dollar-for-dollar investment value, you have some pretty big numbers higher up the food chain. And because they are better financed, they are better able to hide their fraud and/or contest it. But eventually, when you do crack that egg, you can see the seriousness of those dollars. Two percent of the population causes 98 percent of the problems. So you have to go after it in some fashion, but there's only so many dollars to pursue it, so you also have to be very careful in your investment.

ADAM: If you were appointed the secretary of workers' compensation by the president of the United States, what would be the most significant improvements you would make to the system?

DAVID DEPAOLO: [*laughs*] Well, the first thing I would do is ensure that there were minimum standards to be met for each state. This was highlighted by the ProPublica series of articles on workers' compensation and opt-out movement, demonstrating that the loss of an arm in one state might be worth $20,000, but you go across state lines, and it's worth $300,000. And there is very much inconsistency in how wage replacement works, what medical treatment is authorized, usage guidelines, and so forth. So the first thing I would do is establish some mandatory minimums or standards for the provision of workers' compensation benefits.

And then, I think what also needs to be done is better education on what workers' compensation is for both employers and employees. Too many think that workers' compensation involves justice and fairness, and, the fact is, it is neither of those. It's an administrative process that is intended to deliver a certain level of benefits upon the occasion of something bad that happens. Too many people look at it as whether they want justice or it has to be fair. The fact is, that's not the case.

So if I get injured on the job, and let's say I make $150,000 a year, my wage replacement is capped at a very, very low level relative to my wage experience. So is that fair? Of course it's not fair. But that's just the fact of the matter, because it's assumed that I have a greater ability to save money and/or make up that wage replacement later on down the line simply because of my position in life.

By the same token, you might have a very low-wage earner, and in many states, there is a minimum wage-replacement level. So on disability, they can actually make more money than they would…working. And is that fair? No, but that's just the way it is. That's how we decided to operate things. So we just have to come to terms with that. I think if that message gets out to both the employee and employer communities, there is a much better understanding of just what the limitations are.

ADAM: Thank you very much, David.

Chapter 7

Peggy Crook Interview

Peggy Crook is the assistant vice president of claims and loss control for FOJP Service Corporation, which provides risk-management advisory services and administers insurance coverage for a group of hospitals, long-term care facilities, and social-services agencies in the New York City metropolitan area. She is responsible for implementing best practices in workers' compensation claims management and for reducing losses among FOJP's client base. Before joining FOJP in 2012, Peggy was director, global claims for Hilton Worldwide, where she oversaw a $140 million domestic claim program across eight hundred US hotels as well as a global general liability claims program for Hilton's international properties. Peggy's prior experience was at AIG, where she managed AIG's excess-claim unit. Peggy has more than forty years of claims-management experience.

Peggy graduated from the State University of New York with a BS in Business Management and Economics and earned an AIC designation from The Institutes. She is a member of the Marsh Workers' Compensation Advisory Council and is a Claims and Litigation Management Alliance Fellow. She is a past member of the New York State Self Insurers Association Board of Managers and was a member of the Client Risk Advisory Council for a major third-party administrator.

ADAM: Peggy, thank you. What are the top objectives that you are trying to achieve in your role?

PEGGY CROOK: My title is assistant vice president of claims and loss control, so my primary objective with our workers' compensation program for 2016 is to help facilitate the implementation of a solid return-to-work program at our hospital clients. Currently that program is being managed by the hospitals from the ground up, as opposed to the top down, and it is working, but not the way that it could be working. Senior management leadership and ownership are necessary factors for a successful program.

We have two dedicated return-to-work coordinators who are assisting the hospitals with their return-to-work/transitional duty programs. One of the things we are planning to do is hold a return-to-work roundtable discussion with our hospital clients so that they can share information and develop some best practices.

For our agencies and nursing-home clients, my priority is to convince more of those clients to participate in 24/7 nurse triage, which is a best practice, and many of them for a variety of reasons have not fully adopted that as their model for reporting of claims. Those are my two primary objectives for my clients for 2016. There are others, but those are the ones that will have the greatest impact on their experience.

ADAM: What are the best practices that you feel employers should adopt to improve productivity and profits in terms of safety and claims administration? What are some of the challenges?

PEGGY CROOK: That's a great question. I think that if an employer has a culture of safety within their organization, and that is conveyed and felt by their workforce, then profits, profitability, and morale will all go up. It's been shown time and again that if you demonstrate caring for your employees, they will, in turn, care for you. It does trickle down and permeates the organization.

It starts at the top for everything, including safety. One of the challenges that I have seen in my world here is that it does not start at the top; it starts at the bottom. So you may have an entire group who are on board with these principles, but it is very difficult to get it to bubble up to the top, and it's sometimes like an afterthought— "Oh that's a good idea. Let's do it"—as opposed to the CEO saying, "This is my idea, and this is what we will do," and then cascading down through the organization. I've seen that work at other organizations that I have been employed by—that it comes from the top and change is effective.

I guess I answered what are the challenges first. The best practices, again, is senior leadership, the CEO, saying, "This is what we will do." That is them taking accountability and ownership and cascading it down to the levels below. So I think that is the key to the success of any program.

Most organizations of any relative size will have some sort of safety committee that meets on a regular basis. If you don't have a dedicated safety committee, then take an existing committee and either carve out or bolt on a safety component to this committee. Hopefully, participants include some people at the senior level. What I have found with safety committees is that you need line employees involved as well. What I've seen work at other organizations that I have been involved with: take your loudest vocal critics and put them on your safety committee, and they will help effect change and accountability. I've seen that work because they become part of the solution as opposed to pointing out problems.

I think a safety committee is essential, and they can perform a lot of roles. It is very easy for an organization to define that. They can be responsible for root-cause analysis of all incidences, including near misses, because that's how you learn what is driving unsafe behavior that can lead to accidents, or what is actually causing your accidents, so that you can come up with a program to change that. A lot of these may not cost you a dime. It may be as simple as, "OK, we've got an issue. We have employees in a nursing home. We've had thirty fractured pinkies in the last three months. What's going on? OK, let's take a look at how they are moving the patients. Oh, they are doing it wrong." Retraining… costs nothing, fractures disappear. So it could be as simple as that. Also, the safety committee would need to have data so that they can do their trending analysis. So that is on the safety side. Definitely a safety committee, root-cause analysis, training, education, and programs.

I remember years ago, the City of New York Department of Sanitation—I'm going back maybe twenty years—obviously had an issue with back claims with their sanitation workers. They lift all the time, and they had a lot of back claims arising from that. The city instituted fifteen minutes of stretching before each shift, and their back-claim incidents dropped precipitously from a simple warm up exercise. So the employer is out fifteen minutes on a shift, but, in the grand scheme of things, they have healthy employees who are not making claims. So a simple exercise component is important.

On the claims side, there are a few things that everyone should do. Every organization should review their loss runs. They should know who is having accidents, where the losses are occurring, and how much money is being reserved and paid on their claims. They need to validate the data as well, because I've seen instances where there have been errors on loss runs. You've got employees, claimants, being assigned adversely to your experience who is not your employee. The carrier wouldn't know that; the TPA wouldn't necessarily know that; only you would know that, and the way you catch that is by reviewing your loss runs. So you have to understand your numbers; you must. It's not just the premium; the premium is driven in part by your claims experience. You've got to look at that, and, if you don't understand it, ask your TPA or insurer to explain it.

You should schedule claim-review meetings. We are a big advocate of this. We started regular claim-review meetings with our hospital clients two years ago, and what we have found is that it's a great opportunity for educating our clients on the world of workers' compensation here in New York. It helps to understand how things work. It is very different than what you would think if you applied common sense to a situation. We found that the claim reviews were very good ways to educate our clients on the ins and outs of the workers' comp world, discuss strategies to resolve a claim and how to handle it, and identify plans to resolve a particular claim. As they become more educated, they can develop the strategy, and that's where we are at now. Our hospitals are very well educated. They understand Section 32s (settlements), they know LWEC (loss of wage-earning capacity), and they know the workers' compensation acronyms.

One of our medical directors called me about a particular claim. He asked, "Peggy, I've got this employee; she has been out of work almost two years. I might be able to bring her back. Is this something we should try, or should we just let it go and do a Section 32 settlement?" He understands the various different strategies and that same knowledge was learned, in part, through the claim-review process. We started that with our agencies and nursing-home clients two months ago, and we are going to continue that twice a year. I think it will help them to understand how workers' compensation works.

One of the things that we put in place last year with our hospitals, nursing homes, and agencies were 24/7 nurse triage, also called a nurse hotline number. This is a best practice. When I was with another organization, we were one of the early adopters of the 24/7 nurse triage. Initially, when I rolled that program out on a national level, it was a voluntary program. It wasn't mandatory. We got about one-third compliance, which is not a good statistic at all, and not enough to move the needle on your claims.

I went to the president of our organization about the low compliance rate and he said, "That's it. It's now going to be mandatory." It was a fifteen-minute meeting. He drafted a memo—again, top down. "This is now mandatory. Everyone has to comply." So we got our compliance rate up, and the results from that were about one-third of our incidents did not turn into claims.

My previous employer had a lot more rigor around their claims' process. They had a self-insured/high-deductible national program. The group that I am working with now, on the hospital side, essentially had very little rigor around the claims' process. The 24/7 nurse-triage program is new to this hospital group. Organizationally, every hospital has embraced it, and the statistics are off the charts. The numbers are really, really fantastic out of the gate.

I think one of the reasons for that is that the hospital clients are in the business of helping and healing people, so that extends to their employees as well. Yet they had no tools to do anything other than report the claim. That really was it. And they were frustrated. So back to the education piece and the gradual ramping up to the program we have now. They now have tools to help manage and mitigate their losses. It has resulted in claim avoidance. One of our hospital clients has gone completely paperless in the reporting of their workers' compensation claims, which has made their supervisors very happy because that's an administrative burden that has been taken off of them.

The employee is getting attention from a medical professional who's not their employer—an objective medical professional who's not judging them, is only concerned about their injury and determining what the right treatment is for them. The employees like it; the supervisors like it. Everyone's happy. We have reduced the lag time and everyone knows that early reporting keeps your claim costs down. Our claim costs are down. Our lag time is precipitously down, so everything is working.

Regarding compliance, we have one hospital that has a 91 percent compliance rate with 24/7 nurse triage...91 percent! The program is only nine months old. We had one hospital that had 100 percent compliance rate, but a lot of those employees went for medical treatment before they called nurse triage, which they are working to change. The one hospital with a 91 percent compliance rate is the one that is really benefitting. That particular hospital was our worst performing hospital, and they are now the best in this group.

ADAM: To what do you attribute that?

PEGGY CROOK: The education and claim reviews. In addition, two years ago, we had a round-table discussion about return to work, giving examples of other large organizations, and basically saying, "It can be done; other people have done it. Is it easy? It's not easy. You are going to have to work. This is what you need to do." It is a big education and training push, plus support, plus we have in our TPA a good partner who brings a lot to the table.

The hospitals were involved in the selection of the TPA. This was not thrust on them; they were part of the process. They have helped shape their program. They have these tools, steps, and resources, the return-to-work coordinator who is dedicated to their hospital. That's a resource they did not have before; they have that now. All these things have added up to this particular hospital embracing the program.

The other thing that this hospital has, which I think is one of the keys to their success, is they have senior leadership buy-in, big time. So they've got their leadership saying, "Go! Go! Go!" They're just doing a great job! They really are, and it's a very difficult environment.

ADAM: Have you been in situations where there was not leadership buy-in, and were you able to overcome that?

PEGGY CROOK: We are actually in the middle of a situation like that now. First of all, who wouldn't buy into lower costs, happier employees, employees not getting hurt as much? It's really not an argument, it's just a presentation. "This is what it is." Who wouldn't agree with it? Once it is out there, it is not a hard sell.

Some of these organizations are gigantic, and getting to the right people can be difficult, because there are a lot of things on their plate. Workers' compensation is not bubbling up to number one on their plate; it just isn't. What we're trying to do is partner with a senior-level advocate who will advance the cause. It is putting another layer in there, but it's the only way to go, to get that senior-level person to say, "Yes, I get it. I'm going to present to the board. I'm going to get it to the CEO." We are in the midst of that now with one of our clients, managing senior-level buy-in that way.

Others, are sometimes just…"Show me the money. If I do a return-to-work program, how much am I going to save?" It's very hard to quantify that, and if anyone knows of a simple way of doing that, I would love to see it. We have wrestled with that. Intuitively, you know. The studies that say, "Yes, sitting home on the couch is not good for anybody." You are paying for someone to sit on the couch. Still, a lot of the times, you are dealing with financial people who really want to see the return on investment. It is not always easy to quantify that. I wish it was easier, because there are direct costs and indirect costs. And the indirect costs, depending on what you read, can be four to six times the direct costs. So you can say that, but they still want to see the equations.

ADAM: How do you obtain buy-in regarding safety and the focus on safety from management and employees throughout the organization?

PEGGY CROOK: That is the tough one. Again, senior leadership has to advocate for safety. It depends on the organization. I worked for a company that had locations all around the world, and some of those locations had safety committees headed by the general manager in charge of that location. Root-cause analysis was done on a monthly basis; things were fixed. But it was smaller locations, smaller number of employees; that's easily done.

It depends on what your reporting line is for your safety. We have been able to participate in some of the larger institutions that have standing safety committees that address all kinds of safety issues pertaining to the health-care organization. We have been able to bolt on workers' compensation as part of that safety-committee meeting. We rely on them, because we are outside of the organization. We are only advisors, and we can't compel compliance. So we rely on those in the safety committee to take that up the chain. We are trying to bring everyone together so there is one picture, and everyone is on the same page.

ADAM: How important is culture in achieving your objectives, and how do you create and maintain that culture?

PEGGY CROOK: Workplace culture is the key to success in a safety workers' compensation program. This was clearly illustrated with two of our clients in similar business environments. One of these clients has sort of a "gotcha" attitude when it comes to employees. You get the impression that they think their employees are trying to take advantage of them and the system. You get the vibe that they just don't really believe their employees. Not surprisingly, their loss experience is horrible.

Then we have another, larger client, who thinks their employees are great. They value their employees. They have an occupational-health nurse dedicated to taking care of injured employees. They've got safety committees. They've got the bells and whistles, and they always ask "What can we do better?"

The other client, with the not-so-good loss experience, is looking outside to blame outsiders, "You are not handling the claims correctly, and you're not doing this; you're not doing that." They are not looking at themselves. So the larger client, who thinks their employees are great, has a fantastic loss experience. Two different cultures.

The client with the safety culture—we worked very closely with them for more than a year and met with them frequently to refine their workers' comp program. They truly wanted to do better. They wanted better results, and they wanted to do better by their employees. And, they have. But, it starts with them, and with us educating them. We can't force it, but we can educate. Education is very important in changing culture, and it comes from the top, always.

ADAM: What motivates you and your organization to pursue safety?

PEGGY CROOK: The motivation is that it's the right thing to do. I certainly don't want anyone to get hurt doing their job. These are tough jobs these people do.

It wears on them, day after day, year after year. I mean, we have nurses who…they literally get beaten up, literally punched and kicked and bit, pinched and pulled, then kicked and shot at. I mean, they have really bad things happening to them day after day, and they go back to work, year after year.

So, yes, we want them to be safe. We want them to be able to come to work and go home uninjured at the end of the day. What we have put in place here at FOJP this past year is a patient-centered model. The old claims-management model, where you have only independent medical exams (IME) and surveillance in your toolbox, is gone. They are tools, but that is not the beginning and the end. But that's what was here; that's all that was here. It's an entire change, patient-centered, employee-centered model, which resonates with our health-care professionals.

So what motivates me…it's just the right thing to do.

ADAM: How do you measure your results?

PEGGY CROOK: A gazillion reports…

ADAM: Which ones do you feel are the most meaningful?

PEGGY CROOK: I look at the 24/7 nurse-triage stats. So how many losses were taken in? How many called the nurse? How many called the nurse before they got treatment? That's important because, as I said earlier, we had one hospital that had 100 percent of their employees who called the 24/7 nurse-triage line. Great, right? Seventy percent of them had received treatment before they called the nurse; it's a waste of time. The idea of calling the nurse is to do it before you seek treatment, unless it's an emergency.

In looking at who got treatment before they called, we found that some of our clients have occupational-health clinics. Their work flow is, no matter what happens, we want to see the injured employee. It's part of their culture. As a result of looking at those numbers, the occupational-health clinics are no longer seeing employees if the 24/7-hour nurse has directed them for self-care. So they have changed, and we are hoping that those stats will improve even more.

Lag time is another thing I look at. Given the change in NYS Workers' Comp with the "Payor Compliance" and the penalties, it's really essential that our clients report their claims timely. Lag time is very important.

The other statistic I look at is the ratio of indemnity to medical-only claims. That tells me whether or not this program is working, and it is. At the nine-month mark, we flipped our ratios. So one year ago, we had 70 percent of our claims were lost time, 30 percent medical only at the nine-month mark. This year, 70 percent are medical only; 30 percent are lost time. That's not an accident; that's everybody and everything. That's the program working together.

ADAM: Is that your indication that you are running a safer operation?

PEGGY CROOK: Yes, because people are not losing time. They are getting medical treatment; they are staying at work. So that's the big thing. They are either staying at work, or they are maybe losing a day or two, and then are coming right back to work.

It's a multipronged approach to manage a program both preloss, which is the safety side, and includes the 24/7 nurse triage as well, because you can get claim avoidance that way. And then, postloss is your TPA, so it's a multipronged approach where everybody has to work together.

ADAM: Do the processes and strategies used at Hilton achieve similar results at FOJP? Are they universal? If not, why not?

PEGGY CROOK: I think there are some universal best practices. I think the implementation is different; tweaking of the various programs is different. But I think the basics are pretty much the same. It's what kinds of losses are you having? Where are you having them? How do we fix them? Are we addressing them on a regular basis with your safety committees? All of those things are common, really, to everyone.

ADAM: Do you think contests improve safety?

PEGGY CROOK: I really don't. I saw it at Hilton. What I saw worked in the short term. Then there were some claims that were not reported during a certain period, because they wanted to hit their numbers, and so they would hold them back. Maybe some hiding of accidents, some pressure not to report things, some diversion to health care as opposed to workers' comp. I think it is ripe for abuse.

However, I do think healthy competition is a good thing. You may want to keep a scorecard, by department, of who is having the accidents and how many have they had, without a contest, but just as far as information is concerned. We do that with the hospitals. We put them side by side. I will tell you, the competition between them really works. They are very interested in what others are doing and how they stack up. They always ask about it. And it's not a contest; there are no prizes. It's just a healthy competition. I think that works. But contests? I'm not so sure about that.

ADAM: Many employers are suspicious about employee's injuries. How have you overcome that organizationally?

PEGGY CROOK: That's a major culture change. I just keep going back to education. I think it's so important if they understand that at least 80 percent of these are legitimate. Is there fraud? Yes, there is. Outright fraud, staged accidents, I'm not so sure about that. Is there malingering? Yes. It is part of the claim-handling process for them to catch that.

Institutionally, that requires a change in thinking at so many different levels within an organization. That affects morale too, and you can see it in the numbers. Going back to that client with the "gotcha" attitude, just look at their numbers, and you can put it next to another organization just like it.

When I was at Hilton, we had a general manager who was at one of the Hilton hotels in a large city, and that hotel's numbers were through the roof. I had a regional manager at the time, and I asked, "What's going on at…" He said, "I have to figure it out." Long story short, maybe a year later, another hotel in the same city had an increase in claims. I said, "What's going on?" What was happening was the general manager who was at that first hotel went to the next hotel, and that was the change, and their numbers went through the roof.

It was a morale issue. It was how they treat their employees. So for organizations just like that, what ends up happening is they end up paying. Because they have more losses than anyone else, they pay a higher premium. They are difficult cases.

ADAM: Does early return to work in a light-duty capacity improve outcomes?

PEGGY CROOK: There's no question that early return to work improves outcomes. All different kinds of outcomes—financially, obviously, because you are cutting off your total-indemnity payments. That's a huge, huge savings. Plus, you've got the employee who is back at work being productive for you. So they are contributing to your workforce. I don't think you can lose with a return-to-work program.

ADAM: Can you share how you reduced the time it took to report claims from twenty days to two days, and why you focused on that?

PEGGY CROOK: We focused on that, because we know lag time can increase your costs. What we did at Hilton was we measured it. We put it on a scorecard, and the hotels were all listed, and their lag time was shown. They were red, yellow, or green. A typical stop light—everyone understands red, yellow, or green. So if you are in the red, you are bad. Everybody got to see it. They didn't want that; they wanted to be in the green.

So we had a balanced score card, which was three departments. It was safety and security, claims, and human resources. Each department had metrics that we had to follow through on, and we reported all the way up to senior leadership on the scorecard. None of the hotels wanted the president to see them in the red, because they didn't want a phone call from him. It worked. It took a year, but it worked, and it held for a lot of years. Then, the culture changed. The culture was...

you better report this right now, because we don't want to be red.

ADAM: How did you achieve a 30 percent reduction in litigated cases at Hilton?

PEGGY CROOK: That was the early intervention. Early settlement is really what it is. It all flows from early reporting. You find out about it right away, so you handle it right away. People are not discontented; they are satisfied, and information is shared. They understand the process, no need to get an attorney.

ADAM: What do you enjoy most about what you do?

PEGGY CROOK: I think I make a difference, and that, to me, is very important.

ADAM: To what do you attribute your success, and of what achievements are you most proud?

PEGGY CROOK: Well, success...that's not for me to say. It's for others to judge whether I'm successful or not. I just think that I'm very passionate about what I do and what I believe in, and I think that has something to do with being able to achieve things. That's what I attribute it to, being passionate about it.

ADAM: Peggy, thank you so much.

Chapter 8

Jeffrey R. Fenster Interview

Jeffrey R. Fenster is vice president of business development and government affairs at AmTrust Financial Services Inc.

From 2010 until the spring of 2014, Mr. Fenster served as executive director of the New York State Workers' Compensation Board. As executive director, he was responsible for regulation of the second-largest workers' compensation system in the country.

Prior to joining the Workers' Compensation Board, Mr. Fenster was a litigation associate with the New York law firm of Stroock & Stroock & Lavan LLP. While at Stroock, Mr. Fenster represented institutional clients in complex commercial litigations, arbitrations, and federal- and state-government investigations.

He received his bachelor's degree and juris doctorate from the University of Michigan.

ADAM: Jeff, thank you for your participation.

JEFF FENSTER: It's my pleasure.

ADAM: What were your top objectives as the executive director of the New York Workers' Compensation Board, and were they achieved?

JEFF FENSTER: We had tried to look at a system that had gone through a pretty large sea change in 2007. I took over in early 2010, and it had gone through a lot of "reform" with not a lot of tangible improvement from anyone's perspective. Labor was upset; the business community was upset; the insurance community was upset; the government wasn't particularly happy with how things had played out either.

We tried to take a step back, not get into the battles of wage benefit and medical-treatment guidelines, but take a step back and say, "How can the system be improved from what we do?" We are essentially the referee and the operator of the system. "What can we do better to effectuate better interaction between parties and quicker dispute resolution to drive costs down with both efficiency and speed?"

And so we really looked at two sides of that, the medical side of it, and then the dispute-resolution side of it, and tried to begin, and then implement, programs that would do that. Part of that was medical-treatment guidelines, not in the way that I think it was envisioned within the reform, but in a way that quicker medical decisions could be made if there were guidelines and rules around them, and then adding technology to both the dispute-resolution and medical side.

Whether we accomplished them remains to be seen. We certainly didn't accomplish them by the day I walked out the door. I think a lot of them were in motion, and there are a lot of transformative things going on in New York. These are not the things people talk about every day, like capping benefits. There are more technology programs going on behind the scenes, and when they go live, over time, hopefully there will be vast improvements, but it remains to be seen.

The other piece, obviously, that we talked about, that was very important to do, and we did accomplish, was cleaning up the disastrous group self-insurance trust issue. Certainly I would be disingenuous to say I walked in and said, "Let's focus on claims," and things like that, because we had a billion-dollar problem that was affecting thousands of employers in New York and potentially affecting injured workers if they couldn't get paid. I would say we did accomplish the goals there, where we closed that program down and essentially put a mechanism in place to get these employers to pay the debts in an affordable way without bankrupting them and without harming the state's finances. From that perspective, I think that we were successful.

ADAM: What did you enjoy most, and least, about your role at the board?

JEFF FENSTER: The thing I enjoyed most was being in a position in New York State government to really impact people's lives.

Workers' compensation is an important part of the social safety net and an important part of getting certainty when you are running your business. You know that if one of your employees falls, you are not going to have to close your business down next week because there is some judgment against you. At the same time, for employees, if you get injured at work, you know you can take care of your family. That's the goal of it. Being able to hopefully make a small impact on a system that impacts almost every person in the state was the part I enjoyed the most, by far.

I think the least enjoyable part of the job is, without a doubt, the distrust among the various interest groups within the comp system in New York. So labor and business; trial bar, both defense and claimant; and the government too, all of us, I think, had great distrust for each other. I think that continues. It's probably the biggest challenge to improvement that can probably help all those groups—that distrust.

The day-in and day-out dealing with that can be frustrating, because there are ideas that are good out there that could help everybody, but also because one group came up with them, the other group automatically doesn't like them. It makes it difficult, and it certainly slows down the adjudication process. It permeates throughout the whole system. I couldn't quantify it, but I'm sure it's significant, the cost of it to everyone.

ADAM: What are the biggest challenges the board currently faces?

JEFF FENSTER: Certainly that, I think—that is an ongoing challenge.

I think the rising cost of medical, including prescription drugs. This is not a criticism of the board, but I don't think the board, yet, has a great ability to get a handle on the rising cost of prescription drugs and prescription-drug abuse in the system and the rising cost of medical. Even though the medical trend curve is flattening, it's still a significant cost driver and a significant year-over-year cost increase. As the costs continue to go up, there is going to be continued pressure in the system to make significant changes that are difficult.

How these pressures play between the parties is difficult to predict. It's a major challenge for the board, balancing what the statute says and what people are owed, increasing costs and then managing all these interest groups. I think it's, without a doubt, their biggest challenge.

Yet, and at the same time, trying to transform the technology and adjudication infrastructure that was designed and built in the early- to mid-1990s, to transform that into something that works for the future, at the same time that all these external forces with increasing price pressure, premium pressure, and labor angry about the reforms—it's a major challenge.

ADAM: How does the board help employers?

JEFF FENSTER: Well, in an ideal world, the board is someone that employers, or employees, come to when there is a dispute with the employee. The dispute can get resolved very quickly and hopefully get that employee back to work. Now, I think that is a lot easier said than done. Ideally, that's the way the system was intended to work.

The board should be a facilitator of the speed of that process, not a hinderer. They're working to do that, and certainly we started trying to when I was there. They have very good management today that's continuing to try to look at that. I'm not sure all the other interest groups view speed at the board as being a cost saver. They view it as less friction and less annoyance. The board has vision that thinks if things could go faster, particularly in the medical realm, people would go back to work quicker, and the cost would drive down. So I think that is one aspect.

Something they've never gotten any credit for—not to go back to what we talked about before—but in the group self-insurance side, forget about who was to blame; there was a legitimate problem, a one-billion-dollar problem, for employers in the state. I know the employers impacted didn't feel like the board did a lot for them, but I can tell you going through the war with the legislature, going through the war with various other groups that were pushing for different things, employers have gotten a lot, relative to where they were when there was a billion-dollar shortfall, and the state's only option was to literally bankrupt every single one of them.

From that perspective, being a protector of the employer in the marketplace in the last eight to ten years, the board has played a significant role. The reduction in group self-insurance in New York has been only positive, driving business to real insured products or to real self-insurance, where there's real asset posting. From that perspective, employers are much safer in the state with a real security-guarantee fund behind them. Things like that, which didn't exist when 10 percent of the market was probably in group self-insurance.

ADAM: Many employers think the system is stacked against them and that workers' comp is an unfair tax. What are your thoughts?

JEFF FENSTER: I have two thoughts. My first is, I can tell you that I hear the exact same thing from the employee side, that the system is stacked against them; that they don't get what they are due, and it's very difficult to collect; and their employer is always working against them, and the employer doesn't have their best interest at heart, and that's why they need to go to a doctor that has no affiliation with their carrier or employer. So I think both sides have that general sense.

Second, despite the perceived inefficiency in the system, if you look at the initial bargain, it still holds true for employers. Employers are still far better off buying workers' comp insurance and having their employers enter the workers' comp system than having an employee that's injured at work essentially having a tort right against them in every instance. Maybe employers disagree with that, but I think that would be mass chaos, at least in New York. I can't speak as much for every other state. Undoubtedly, it would be more expensive. I think the comp system does contain costs for employers.

Now, I don't doubt that employers wish they contained costs more, and premiums have gone up in New York fairly significantly since the reform. Part of that's probably because the reform might have overpromised on cost savings, and part of that is because some of the cost saving that people legitimately thought would have come to fruition just haven't. I can understand the perspective, but I don't think we've reached a point where the bargain still doesn't hold, where employers are better off saying, "I'll go on my own, and let them sue me in Supreme Court, and we'll see how it goes."

ADAM: How has the board become more effective at fighting fraud?

JEFF FENSTER: Well, there are a couple of things. The board has spent a lot of time building up a fairly good technology platform on proof of coverage and linking Department of Labor data and insurance-company data in pretty close to real-time overnight transfer, seeing what employers in New York State aren't covered and getting them covered. They have a lot of power now, stop-work orders and such.

If you looked at the numbers—I haven't looked at them in two years—the percentage of employers that are operating above the table, so that they are reporting to the Department of Labor but don't have coverage, has gone down significantly. I think that number is less than 5 percent of the state now, and at some point, it was well above 10 percent. Certainly, from the perspective of "we're just not going to participate in the system" kind of employers, that's been greatly reduced.

Fraud, to me, has a lot of different aspects of it. On the medical side, I think there is a lot of fraud in the doctor community. If you looked at the last five or six years, the board has probably removed more doctors from their authorized list than probably any time in their history. I believe as they continue to expand the data reporting within medical, in a way that's going to be easier for the doctor but also more meaningful for the board. They are going to have the ability to really dig into what doctors are doing. Part of the vision, at least it was when I was there, was that a new system would be able to detect medical fraud by the claimant or by the doctor on a more systematic basis. That's coming, and I think that it's going to be a big change.

I focus on the doctor more than the claimant on the medical side, because a claimant is one claimant, but if you get a doctor who treats four thousand injured workers a year, and they are committing fraud on every case, that's an enormous cost to the system. A relatively small percentage of doctors are causing a large percentage of the medical waste in the system. The board is looking to make improvements in that area.

As far as claimant fraud, which is generally what employers talk about, my perspective is it's much more of a gray area. The current system for dealing with employee fraud is really through the adjudication process. Employers would argue that that hasn't been effective, that things happen in cases and it's clear fraud, and nothing happens. There have been some relatively high-profile prosecutions and high-profile cases. But there has not been a systematic focus on how we can weed out employee fraud. I never saw, when I was at the board, convincing evidence that there was a widespread employee-fraud problem. I think it was more of a "lawyers pushing the envelope" problem in particular cases. That wasn't clear fraud.

It is an ongoing discussion in the industry, and certainly in New York and at the board, of what role should the board play in that, and how important is it, and how much of a problem is it? A lot of the study done on this by industry groups has been subpar. They haven't produced the kind of evidence you would like to see to say, "OK, this is a real problem." Whereas you look at the opioid problem in workers' comp, and if you look at the studies done by WCRI or others, it's pretty clear; the evidence is stark. We looked at the employee-fraud evidence that comes out, and I don't think it's as stark.

ADAM: From your perspective, what are employers doing right and wrong?

JEFF FENSTER: So I guess I would answer this question a couple of ways. One is, in my old role, I spoke to a lot of multistate employers, big employers that had employees in a large number of jurisdictions, so they had experience in comp systems in the jurisdictions. They all said, "Our experience in XYZ state is so much better than New York. Why can't we make New York like that?"

If you are coming to New York, and you think the system that works in "pick your state" should work here, you are going to be disappointed, because going back to the distrust we talked about among parties doesn't lead to the more trusting comp systems where everyone plays together. Then, when there is a dispute, the comp board in that particular state steps in a very small percentage of cases. I've never met anyone in New York who thinks that system can actually be implemented in New York. It's nice to think about. I look at some of the states that I think have very good systems, and I wish New York had those systems, but I'm not sure they are implementable here, at least today.

I think there is a lot of lip service in the employer community paid to safety. I know you spend a lot of your time and a lot of time of your company with your employers on safety, and I think it's great. But I think most employers in New York maybe pay lip service but don't really focus on reducing accidents and actually getting people back to work, have meaningful light-duty programs, and things like that. Quite honestly, the state would like them to do it, but there hasn't been a great move to actually effectuate that other than just saying, "We think you should have these programs."

I don't think employers fully have committed to drug-free workplaces, safety programs, and return-to-work programs. I don't think it's because those things wouldn't be economically effective; I don't think there's some evil calculation employers have done and said, "It is better if people leave, and we'll just pay our premiums." I think it takes a real commitment by management. Running a business, it's busy, and there are a lot of things—sitting down and really committing to the safety part of it can be challenging. But a lot of employers would really benefit from doing it, not just in New York, but nationally. Relatively small improvements in injury rates and small improvements in getting people back to work quicker, as opposed to having them out on temporary or permanent disabilities, would be significant for a lot of employers. I think there is not a huge focus on it.

ADAM: Do you think employers' participation in group self-insured trusts is a good risk-management strategy in a state with a competitive workers' compensation market?

JEFF FENSTER: I think there are a couple of self-insured groups in the state where it makes a lot of sense. Discrete industries or discrete groups of employers and employees that are banding together do make some sense.

But in 99-point-something percent of the cases, an employer is far better off either being in an insured program or being in a true self-insured program, where you are self-insured, but you're reporting your losses, and you're posting dollars to support those losses. That should only be for the biggest employers, of course. By the biggest, I really mean the biggest. Everyone else should be in a true insured program.

I think the evils of self-insurance have been pretty clear in the last decade in New York. I think folks, probably like yourself, have noticed it long before the last decade. As rates go up, there will probably be a growing chorus to reopen group self-insurance in New York. I hope people don't forget about the damage and wreckage it caused. It's kind of quiet now. Some employers are still complaining, and it's for the most part contained, but it can be incredibly damaging with very perverse incentives. It can be scary.

The other thing I'll add is there's group self-insurance for municipalities today. When I was at the board, that was always very concerning to me as well. We spent a lot of time with those folks, because as scary as it is to start seeing employers go out of business because of group self-insurance, if mass municipality bankruptcies started happening because of group self-insurance, that would be even scarier. It is certainly a risk factor when I look at the comp system in New York. With group self-insurance among municipalities, there is a significant risk out there today.

ADAM: Why does workers' compensation reform rise to one of the top platform positions for many governors?

JEFF FENSTER: It's because it's important to employers, and it is important to the progressive and labor side of the aisle too. They have vigorous disagreements, and they almost are always in the governor's office from day one, telling him, "This is incredibly important to us, and we need you to fix it." Governors almost always have to respond to that. In New York, it's probably approaching $8 billion for our economy, so it's not insignificant from that perspective either. The size and the loud screaming from all the interest groups lead governors to say, "Something does have to be done." Plus, there is obviously and clearly inefficiency in the system that people feel could be fixed.

ADAM: Why is it so difficult to effect change?

JEFF FENSTER: For one, the approach of significant change through legislation has not been overly successful. Regulatory or process change, if the groups could focus on it, would be probably more successful, where you get people who are experts in how the processes work and how things play out. When things have been done with the legislature, they're done with good intention, but how they flow through the system and ultimately play out in terms of the incentives in the system is not always understood when the legislations pass. It has led to some failures in the system.

The obvious example is you look at the expectation of the number of cases per year that would be capped after the 2007 reform, and I don't know exactly, but my guesses were more than 50 percent less than that today. We're capping less than 50 percent of the cases we assumed we would cap—we being New York State and the whole system—in the reform, which is just driving cost based on an estimate we had. We had a point estimate, and that estimate has been wrong.

That leads people to say, "OK, we need to change more and more." It builds upon itself. You do a reform; it doesn't work; you need to do more reform. Until we get to a place where the cost structure is both acceptable to the majority of the employer community and it's stable, where you aren't seeing rates going way up or way down, there's going to be always cries for more reform. If you see rates start going down, the labor side is going to say, "Well, we need to get more of a piece of the pie back." If rates continue to rise, like they are, the employer communities continue to say, "We never got our bargain."

Until there is stabilization, the governor is always going to be in the middle, trying to effectuate that stabilization. Ultimately, the two sides, while they have to come to agreement for the system to operate, have diametrically opposite interests sometimes. Sometimes I think that they don't—they think they're opposed to each other, but they really could find compromise. But on issues like, "What should your lost-wage benefit be?"—there may not be a lot of compromise there. So I think those things lead to ineffective reform.

No doubt—I would be remiss if not saying it—that neither side trusts the Workers' Comp Board or the government very much, and that makes it hard for the government or the Workers' Comp Board to effectuate meaningful change, because one side or the other will always accuse them of, "Well, you're just in the pocket of one or the other." The board, in my experience, was, and is, the objective arbiter; it really had no interest other than trying to make it work.

ADAM: In 2006, before the 2007 workers' compensation reforms were enacted, New York was ranked the tenth highest in terms of cost in the nation. According to the 2014 report by the Oregon Department of Consumer and Business Services, New York's workers' compensation cost rose to the fourth highest in the nation. In your opinion, what remains to be done to bring costs down?

JEFF FENSTER: There are some deficiencies in the Oregon report. I'm not attacking Oregon, because it is not a deficiency for Oregon. If my memory serves me right, they calculate cost by applying the Oregon employee mix to every other state. I'm not suggesting that's right or wrong, but let's say it's fourth.

There has been a lot of movement in a lot of other states in the last ten years to do significant cost-reducing reforms, but not much for the employee. New York hasn't taken that approach. New York has tried to do reforms that have had a little bit for everyone. So it is not surprising that New York hasn't fallen down the list when other states are enacting cost-saving changes. But New York also has probably one of the worst opioid problems in the comp system in the country. As that continues to fester, our rates are going to continue to go up to support that, and, like we know, the reform savings haven't really occurred in the terms of capping yet.

With respect to what remains to be done to bring costs down, I shouldn't say it's simple. There are two pieces to it: there's the indemnity and the medical. The indemnity cost increases are generally being driven by increasing duration, and as long as duration continues to increase, as long as there are motivations in the system to not to go back to work, to continue to be disabled, where there's minimal incentive to get to maximum medical improvement, you are going to continue to see the duration go up. My guess is duration is up significantly, even since the 2007 reform.

On the medical side, medical and comp are always interesting. There is a medical-cost problem in the country and an overall system that comp can't really control as much as it would like. Comp seems to do marginally worse than the rest of the system. There is a big opioid problem in the country, and it's kind of exacerbated within comp because, by definition, our population is injured, frequently significantly. So getting a handle on the medical problem is more of a national issue that we hope will trickle to comp. There are things that can be done within the comp system, in terms of medical fraud like I talked about earlier, and speed and efficiency of treatment. Honestly, a lot of it, on the medical side, is going to be at the margins until the overall medical inflation problem is controlled in this country.

ADAM: What changes would New York need to make in order to become the national leader in workers' compensation?

JEFF FENSTER: That is a tricky question. Like I said before, things that work in a lot of other states just don't work here because of the distrust among the parties and the strength of the interest groups on both sides.

I happen to believe strongly, and not everyone agrees with me, that if the board was simply the arbiter of dispute and not the hub of the entire wheel of workers' comp, where every piece of paper and every single nod and approval had to go to them, the system would operate much more efficiently. If the board set clear—which I believe they are trying to do—performance targets for actors in the system, and then held those actors to those targets, the system would be a national model. Among the nice things about the New York Workers' Comp Board and system is they have the resources to implement those things, and they're trying to. Whereas in other states—I used to speak to a number of these states—they didn't have the resources to implement the operational changes that they would need to do.

From my perspective, reducing conflict and becoming just a conflict arbiter would go a long way to getting to where we need to be. That's a huge sea change from where we are today, though. That's something that probably happens over a decade or two, with significant pain, because people are used to the system and probably profit off of the inefficiency of the system—many actors, not all.

ADAM: What do you see changing in workers' compensation over the next few years in New York and nationally?

JEFF FENSTER: The board has a pretty significant technology project that they are working on, and I expect that they'll roll that out over the next several years.

The national issues are interesting, in terms of opt-out and the attacks on the constitutionality of workers' compensation in certain states. I don't see that coming to New York in the near term, but I could be wrong, I've been wrong before. But I don't think we have reached that point in New York where the interest groups are ready to throw in the towel on the system. The system being $8 billion, a lot of people are making a lot of money in the system, and they are not quite ready to say, "Let's blow it up," like they are in some other states.

In New York, you'll see steady improvement that probably won't make anyone happy on the regulatory side and the operational side from the board. In the legislature, you'll see minimal improvement. I don't think you're going to see the legislature do wholesale comp reform. I don't want to speak for the legislature, but I feel like they have some comp fatigue. The interest groups are pretty far apart on the current issues that people are talking about, and it would be surprising to me if something very significant happened. I wouldn't count out my former colleagues, because they do a great job, and they could potentially get some significant reforms done. But it's definitely going to be a challenge given the opposition at the moment.

Nationally, in some ways, workers' compensation is under attack. In a lot of states—Florida, Oklahoma, and Texas—there's a real battle going on in those states. In Tennessee, whether workers' compensation is the best way for employers to mitigate their exposure to their employees getting injured at work. In Florida, whether comp is the best way for employees to get compensated for their injuries at work. It's going to be interesting to see how those are going to play out and to see if they catch on in other states or not.

Additionally, I mentioned it a number of times, the opioid crisis is pretty tragic, and it takes what could be a minor or less debilitating injury and ruins people's lives. It is bigger than comp, but within comp, it is really significant, and it is destroying people's lives that enter our system, and then really never leave. That is the national issue that needs to be dealt with, certainly in New York, but also elsewhere.

ADAM: If you were reappointed the executive director of the Workers' Compensation Board tomorrow, what would you do differently?

JEFF FENSTER: Well, I would resign on my second day. That would be the first thing [*laughs*].

That's a good question. I was at the board more than four years. I did five executive budgets. It took me a long time to get good communication and good trust among all the interest groups.

If I could go back to my twenty-nine-year-old self and say, "Here's how you should do it from the beginning," I would have spent more time in my first year sitting with the interest groups, alone, and trying to understand exactly what they wanted. Now that may have done no good, but it took me until years two and three to really have the folks in those groups that I could talk to and understand where they were and have the mutual respect. More good could have been done if I had done that quicker. That is what I would say, in terms of what I would do differently, if I could to do it again.

ADAM: How has your perspective of the workers' compensation system changed since working for an insurance company?

JEFF FENSTER: That's interesting. When I was at the board, I had basic assumptions about what was important to insurance companies and employers from a claims-process perspective and what was problematic and what wasn't.

Some of those assumptions have proved to not be true. I always had a sense that insurance companies never wanted to pay or settle, because they would have to lay out money, and it was a draw on reserves and capital. Talking to our claims people, who are excellent, they are really trying to settle cases as quickly as possible. That wasn't something that I necessarily understood when I was at the board. The insight I've gained working for an insurance company has definitely improved my understanding of the system. If I were to go back, it would be very beneficial as to how I did my job.

ADAM: Is workers' compensation a profitable business?

JEFF FENSTER: For AmTrust, it certainly is.

It's a business that requires you to have a laser-like focus in underwriting and claims handling and on expenses. You have to watch your expenses, you have to be very careful of what you underwrite, and you have to be very diligent on how you manage claims. Things can get out of control if you don't do all three of those things. But if you do, and AmTrust and other companies do it, it can be a profitable line to write. I think AmTrust has a niche subset of the comp business. We're very proud of it, and it's a very profitable subset of the comp business.

I think if you enter the comp market and you say, "I will write anything, and I'll outsource my claims handling, and it will be OK," I think you are going to be in some trouble, probably significant trouble. But if you do things in a very disciplined manner, it definitely can be. That's probably true of most lines.

ADAM: Of what are you most proud?

JEFF FENSTER: Other than my baby daughter and my wife, I'm proud to have served the people of New

York for five executive budgets and worked with an incredible team at the Workers' Comp Board, promoted a lot of folks at the board, and left behind a group of people who are very talented and skilled. The people at the board are among the most dedicated civil servants I know. I'm just proud to the extent I have made any impact, had the opportunity to.

I'm proud that I served two governors, worked as hard as I could, gave them everything I had, and tried to improve the system to the greatest extent possible.

People kind of joke about public service, but I felt very strongly that it is important spending time in public service. To the extent people complain about the government and they don't like how things are operated, the only way that gets improved is if talented people go into government. Clearly, I haven't made an entire career of it, but I've spent my time, and I may spend more time in the future in government. The more talented people who go into government, the more our government will be responsive to our needs and solve our problems. It is important to do that.

So I'm proud to have served New York for the time I did. Hopefully, I made some people's lives better and put the board on a decent trajectory. Hopefully, things will continue to improve in this system moving forward.

ADAM: Is there anything you would like to add?

JEFF FENSTER: No, you asked a lot of excellent questions. The comp system in New York especially, but nationally, is challenging. It is a challenging line. It is a challenging system for the employee to navigate, and it's a challenging and frustrating system for the employer.

It is important to remember, and I said it before, it's much better than the alternative, what we had in the early 1900s. What that system would be like today, in our current litigation environment, it would be a nightmare. It would be crippling to our economy. One of the fun things about comp is it's always striving to improve, with all the people in it trying to make it better, not always in the same direction.

ADAM: Jeff, thank you so much.

Chapter 9

The Chief Caring Officer (CCO)

In December 2014, in pursuit of a lifelong dream, I sailed a forty-five-foot Outremer catamaran with Captain Jan Cluistra and two crewmates across the Atlantic Ocean from France to the Caribbean. Having courageously crossed the ocean just under forty times, Captain Jan Cluistra is the epitome of a leader who cares and takes personal responsibility for people's safety. Our lives depended on it.

Leading by example, Captain Jan proactively addressed whatever might put us at risk. He vigilantly checked the weather, boat, and equipment for potential failure and the morale and well-being of the crew. Jan considered any question a good question and welcomed suggestions on sail selection and trim, but anything that he felt jeopardized our safety was nonnegotiable.

Sailing safely to the other side of the ocean was Captain Jan's purpose. He required safe behavior and functioning equipment as a "precondition, not a goal."[6] We practiced climbing the mast and reefing sails in calm seas so that we would be prepared and confident in storm conditions. His caring and calm leadership fueled our confidence and instilled a culture of teamwork, mutual trust, and respect. By reducing risk, we were unburdened by fear, which allowed us to thoroughly enjoy our wonderful crossing.

Captain Jan is an "enlightened leader,"[7] our chief caring officer (CCO), the kind of leader I aspire to be, and the kind of leader with whom I was so grateful to sail.

The "root cause" of safety in the workplace is the culture. The "root cause" of the culture is the leader. Like Captain Jan, the leader must be the chief caring officer and look after people who work at the company as if their lives depend upon it—because, in some organizations, they do.

Many management books suggest hiring great people, getting "the right people on the bus."[8] One of the goals of this book is to share strategies that *keep* "the right people on the bus." Optimal performance requires that healthy and happy people are productively and safely working.

Safety can be a nebulous concept. How and where do you begin to implement safety, and how is it measured? Fortunately, Paul O'Neill's "zero injuries" strategy

---

6 Paul O'Neill's phrase.

7 Bill O'Rourke's phrase.

8 Collins, *Good to Great*, 13.

brings much needed clarity. By aspiring to make "zero injuries"[9] happen, the CCO will empower employees, both physically and emotionally, with a clearly defined, measurable destination.

The following thoughts from the interviews highlight the critical role of leadership. According to Paul O'Neill, "I think the culture of an organization is a consequence of the actions of the person in charge.[10] You need to have a mind-set that says, 'If I'm in charge, it's my responsibility to make sure you're safe.'[11] Safety is a leading indicator of all performance at an institution. If you know what the safety performance is, you can be pretty sure that the rest of the performance is not better than the safety performance.[12] Every organization is a function of the alignment of energy of the people who are in it."[13]

Bill O'Rourke shares, "I believe it's an enlightened leader's responsibility to protect the health and well-being of all employees.[14] The leader's responsibility is to create the kind of climate where employees can thrive, learn, develop, and become better people. And one of the roots of that kind of enlightened leadership is

---

9   Paul O'Neill's strategy.
10 Page 10.
11 Page 11.
12 Page 17.
13 Page 9.
14 Page 20.

treating your employees, all of them, with dignity and respect, and a form of that is safety."[15]

Stephen Newell also sums it up well: "I've been in this profession for forty years, and to me, safety is a hearts-and-minds profession. Any employer can direct their employees to do a job or a task, and they will comply. However, most of us realize that if people really care about what they're doing, they will do a better job, and they will put more of themselves into it. To me, caring is a reciprocal property. It would be hard for me to care about a business if I felt the business didn't care about me. And so I think health and safety is a key ingredient to business success.[16] The safety culture is created by the leadership at the top of the organization."[17]

Brian Connor adds, "If you ask any employer what they value most from their employees, I think most employers would value loyalty among the highest of qualities. By treating people as disposable, there is no loyalty there."[18]

David DePaolo says, "It just comes down to one single thing: that's your employee. If you…demonstrate to the employee…that you care…you're going to end up with a more productive employee."[19]

Jeff Fenster adds, "Relatively small improvements in injury rates and small improvements in getting people

---

15   Page 21.
16   Page 59.
17   Page 60.
18   Page 81.
19   Page 93.

back to work quicker, as opposed to having them out on temporary or permanent disabilities, would be significant for a lot of employers."[20]

Peg Crook shares, "I think that if an employer has a culture of safety within their organization, and that is conveyed and felt by their workforce, then profits, productivity, and morale will all go up. It's been shown time and again that if you demonstrate caring for your employees, they will, in turn, care for you. It does trickle down and permeate the organization. It starts at the top for everything, including safety. The best practice, again, is senior leadership, the CEO saying, 'This is what we will do.' That is them taking accountability and ownership and cascading it down to the levels below. So I think that is key to the success of any program."[21]

The inspiring leaders in this book share a unique passion for their work and a genuine care for the well-being of others. But even if you don't have the same degree of passion for safety, you can still focus on making "zero injuries" happen and, consequently, unleash productivity and profits. Be the chief caring officer, the new CCO, and lead your people and organization to excellence.

---

20 Page 133.
21 Page 104.

Appendix

Leverage the Experience Modification

To capture some of the financial benefits of safety, it's important to understand how experience modifications reward employers who have safe environments and practices for their workforce and penalize employers with unsafe acts and conditions.

Employers purchase insurance to transfer risk to an insurance company. However, the experience modification of premium can undermine that transfer, because it can retroactively charge an employer's workers' compensation policy for prior claims.

The experience modification is calculated by comparing an employer's actual claims to their expected claims based on their payroll and industry classification codes. If an employer's actual claims are more than expected, an additional premium is charged due to a debit experience modification factor greater than 1.00, and if they are less than expected, there's a reduction in premium due to a credit experience modification factor less than 1.00.

Experience modifications are calculated annually by the New York Compensation Insurance Rating Board regardless of which carrier insures the employer. Outside of New York, the National Council of Compensation Insurance and other independent bureaus calculate annual experience modifications.

Effective in October 2015, New York caught up with the rest of the country by including the first $15,000 as primary losses. The formula discounts the impact of claims over $15,000. Prior to October 2013, the formula discounted claims over $5,000. The changes increased employers' experience modifications and premiums.

Each employee's workers' compensation claim is included in three years of experience modification calculations. For example, an experience modification effective in 2016 includes the claims that occurred in 2014, 2013, and 2012. The prior year, 2015 in this example, is not included in the calculation.

As you can see in the chart below, a claim that occurred in the 2014 policy year is included in three years of experience modification calculations (2016, 2017, and 2018). The 2014 claim will no longer modify premiums starting in the 2019 policy year.

	Experience Modification Year		
	2016	**2017**	**2018**
Year	**2014**	2015	2016
Claim	2013	**2014**	2015
Occurred	2012	2013	**2014**

The chart below shows the cumulative three-year premium charges as a percentage of various claims.

Three-Year Premium Cost of Various Claims

Claim Amount	$10,000 Premium	$500,000 Premium	$1,000,000 Premium	$3,000,000 Premium
$500	53%	270%	240%	360%
$1,000	53%	270%	270%	360%
$5,000	53%	270%	276%	288%
$10,000	53%	272%	276%	288%
$50,000	18%	119%	140%	185%
$100,000	10%	87%	110%	164%

Notice that the charge for each claim increases as an employer's premium increases. For example, on a policy with a $10,000 premium, a $1,000 claim will cost the employer 53 percent or $530, or $176.67 extra premium paid annually for three years, due to the claim's increasing of the experience modification. A larger employer with the same $1,000 claim but a $3 million policy premium will pay 360 percent, or $3,600, in additional premium over three years.

The employer with a $1 million premium is charged more than the actual claim, even on larger claims of $100,000. Risk is only transferred on claims that increase after the claim is too old to be included in the calculation. For example, changes in a 2012 claim will not impact an experience modification effective after 2016.

Unfortunately, the situation is even worse than it appears. When claims are reported, the insurance company reserves money for the estimated cost. The amount of the estimate, or reserve, is used in the experience modification calculation and is frequently higher than the final amount paid. For example, a claim that ultimately costs $3,000 could have an average estimated reserve of $5,000 during the three years it was included in the calculation. On a $500,000 premium, the employer would pay 270 percent, or $13,500 in additional premium (over the next three years), for a claim that only ultimately cost $3,000 when treatment concluded.

To be fair, estimating the ultimate cost of injuries and illnesses is certainly not an exact science. In our experience, the costs of most claims are overestimated. However, those that are underreserved are so significantly underestimated, especially for back injuries, that in the aggregate, claims are underreserved.

Employers should know what their minimum experience modification could be if they had zero claims for the three years included in their experience modification calculations. The difference between an employer's current experience modification and their potential minimum is their "controllable"[22] experience modification. The controllable modification illustrates the maximum potential savings, before any additional savings from premium discounts or dividends are applied, assuming no claims in the three years included in the calculation.

Premium

before Mod.	$10,000	$500,000	$1,000,000	$3,000,000
Current Mod.	1.20	1.20	1.20	1.20
Current Premium	$12,000	$600,000	$1,200,000	$3,600,000
Minimum Mod.	0.93	0.64	0.57	0.43
Minimum Premium	$9,300	$320,000	$570,000	$1,290,000
Controllable Mod.	0.27	0.56	0.63	0.77
Controllable Savings	$2,700	$280,000	$630,000	$2,310,000

---

22 Data from ModMaster Mod Analysis by Zywave Inc.

The chart above assumes that each premium had a current 1.20 debit experience modification because the actual claims exceeded what was expected. For example, if an employer had a premium of $500,000 with a 1.20 current experience modification in 2016, the premium would be $600,000 ($500,000 × 1.2 = $600,000). With zero claims in 2014, 2013, and 2012, the minimum experience modification would have been 0.64, and the net premium would have been only $320,000 ($500,000 × 0.64 = $320,000). The "controllable savings" would have been $280,000 ($600,000 − $320,000 = $280,000) plus any discounts or dividends offered due to the great claims experience.

The strategy is to improve safety and capture some, or all, of your "controllable savings." Some of the projected savings can be used to invest in safety training and new equipment to generate additional savings and productivity. Look at it optimistically: savings will be captured as you improve safety, even if you don't achieve zero injuries.

The leader must create a culture of caring and safety to eliminate injuries and keep your "A-team" of employees working and safe. Let the experience modification savings help motivate your team to go for zero injuries. The financial benefits will follow.

With Gratitude

Thank you to all of the wonderful people in this book for generously sharing your time, insights, and passion for improving people's lives.

While doing research for this book, I learned that Paul O'Neill's consulting firm, Value Creation LLC, was holding a seminar on safety in Pittsburgh. I thoroughly enjoyed the two days with Mr. O'Neill and Bill O'Rourke and their excellent team and highly recommend it. I am especially grateful to Mr. O'Neill for kindly sharing his exceptional ideas. His participation helped attract other outstanding industry leaders to share their unique insights. I thank you all.

I would like to thank the following people for their help and contribution in writing the book and crafting questions for the interviews. First, I am very grateful for Theresa Picco for being a sounding board and for her editorial assistance, ideas, and insightful questions. Further, I would like to thank Cosmo Preiato,

Joe Fasciglione, Mike Peragine, Ray Sullivan, Cecelia Cospito, Dan Stangarone, and Alex Giarrusso and the rest of my teammates for reading and making recommendations to improve the book.

I thank the ACK Board, comprising Richard Anfang, Brian Stuckelman, and Barry Bohrer, for their many years of guidance and wisdom. Also, thanks to Arthur Natter, Dan Abt, Peter Samaha, Martin Green, Jon McHugh and Captain Jan Cluistra for helping make this happen.

I would like to thank my parents, Bert and Judy, for their endless love, encouragement and support.

Finally, thank you to Lisa, my wonderful wife and best friend, for her love and support, and to my awesome son and daughter, David and Allie. You give joy meaning.

About the Author

Adam Friedlander is the president of Friedlander Group Inc., the workers' compensation leader in New York. Adam started his career in insurance in 1983, after graduating from the University of Denver and Rye Country Day School.

Friedlander Group manages seven workers' compensation safety groups that have saved members over $400 million in premiums. Friedlander Group also manages the Workers' Care Group, which helps non-safety group clients improve safety and unleash productivity and profits.

In 2011, Adam published *How to $ave Big on Workers' Compensation*. Adam wrote several published articles on the inherent risks of group self-insured workers' compensation trusts.

Contact Information:

Friedlander Group Inc.
2500 Westchester Avenue
Suite 400
Purchase, New York 10577
www.friedlandergroup.com

914-694-6000 extension 206
Email: adamf@friedlandergroup.com
Book Blog: https://safetyandworkerscomp.com/
First Book Blog: www.howtosavebigonworkerscomp.com
http://www.linkedin.com/in/friedlanderadam
Twitter: @friedlanderadam

Made in the USA
Middletown, DE
29 August 2016